DR. AART BONTEKONING

THE POWER OF GENERATIONS

THE POWER OF GENERATIONS

HOW TO KEEP AGING ORGANIZATIONS UP TO DATE

THE DUTCH CASE

DR. AART BONTEKONING

Warden Press

© 2017 Aart Bontekoning

ISBN:
Paperback: 978-94-92004-51-2
E-book (Epub): 978-94-92004-52-9
E-book (Kindle): 978-94-92004-53-6

This is an extended and updated edition of the Dutch
original publication, *Nieuwe generaties in vergrijzende
organisaties* (Amsterdam: Mediawerf, 2014).

Design and lay-out: Akimoto, Amersfoort

This edition published by Warden Press, Amsterdam.

Table of contents

Preface   7

1. Down to the heart of the matter   8

2. Towards a generational theory   14

3. Generational shifts in the Netherlands   26

4. The Dutch Protest Generation as a new   42
generation of vital seniors

5. The Connecting Generation X in the   30
phase of leadership

6. The Pragmatic Generation: an   50
inhibited, yet accelerating generation

7. The Authentic Generation Y as potential   60
pattern innovators

8. The Conscious Generation Z, children   70
of pragmatic parents

9. Differences between generations in   78
terms of social media use

10. Social evolution in the Netherlands in   86
the twenty-first century

11. A summary of essentials, three matters   96
of discussion and suggestions for future
generation research

Appendix – Towards a scientific   101
method for generational research

Literature   107

About the author   110

Preface

About 85 % of Dutch and other European organizations are aging. Over the next two decades, the number of people in the oldest Dutch working generations will exceed those in the youngest ones. Many other European countries are facing the same effects, risks and opportunities of an aging working population. In the Netherlands, aging will hit its peak at most companies around 2035.

Aging organizations are at risk of falling behind in keeping their organizational culture up to date. This insidious process of getting out of date is creeping in and undermining organizations' ability to survive in a changing world. From a generational perspective, surprising new ways can be found to keep an aging organization (culture and processes) in good social, economic and ecological health.

I do not deny the importance of looking at individuals; that perspective allows us to identify unique talents and find ways to support these talents in order to stimulate individual development. The development of a vital and healthy culture depends on the evolutionary power of successive generations. The intensity and quality of interaction between generations generate the speed of the evolution of the culture of which they are a part.

Working with the generation approach in an organization or another social system asks for a willingness to change the culture from the inside out, from within the professional heart of an organization. This evolutionary process is driven by a coaching leadership style.

The generation approach is also connected to sustainability. The focus is on stimulating every generation to do what creates most energy (at work). When people work in a way that energizes them, they learn to recharge their 'human battery' all the time. This will extend the durability of their 'human battery' and of their working life.

This book is based on more than twenty years of ongoing scientific generational research at many Dutch companies in all kind of industries, and on some research in other European countries and in Brazil.

I owe many thanks to all those companies in many different industries where I was allowed to implement my generational approach. I thank all the participants in generation projects, master classes and workshops for their feedback and support.

I would also like to thank Lotte Visser for her support in translation, Audry Bron for her supervision, and Jessica Mills, Robbert van Kempen, David Ward and Suzanne Merritt for reading the final versions of this book and for their feedback.

Haaren, November 11th, 2017.
Aart Bontekoning

1 Down to the heart of the matter

People who live or work together consciously and unconsciously create their own unique culture. They interactively select social patterns such as ways to communicate, collaborate, lead, learn, think, deal with emotions, diversity and so on, which ultimately become distinguishing features of their community. To keep their culture in good health, these patterns need to be updated from time to time. Like food, social patterns that people create and repeat have an expiration date. In order to keep their culture in good social, economic and ecological health, outdated social patterns need to be replaced by up-to-date ones. The longer you leave a social pattern unchanged after its expiration date, the more human vitality and human energy will drain away, and the more life threatening it will become for the working community. Aging organizations are at high risk at this point. Successive generations and the interaction between older and younger generations play a key role in these evolutionary culture-updating processes. The motor of culture redesign processes is the survival instinct of every working generation. Many aging organizations and institutions in the Netherlands and across Europe need the evolutionary power of new generations more than ever to stay up to date in a fast-changing world. Note that I used the word 'new' instead of 'young'! The demographic reality in today's aging Europe is that our economic, social and ecological future depends on the youthfulness of all (working) generations. Generations are made up of peers who were born within a time span of fifteen years, and generations succeed each other in the various life phases (fig. 1). The potential 'culture-updating power' lies in the differences between one generation and the next in a life phase. Each new generation, from the oldest to the youngest, has the potential power to contribute to the culture's updating processes. Each generation is by nature, consciously or unconsciously, focused on renewing/regenerating another part of their surrounding culture. This power can be found in the area that generates most of their energy (at work). You have to look for it to see it; you have to DO it to experience the real effects at work.

New generations in next phase of life >
their energizers are updates in own culture

Generation = cluster born within a 15-year time span

Consious generation	Authentic generation (1985 - 2000)	Pragmatic Generation (1970 - 1985)	Connecting generation (1955 - 1970)	Protest Generation (1940 - 1955)	Silent generation

Life phases at work = clusters of 15 years of age.

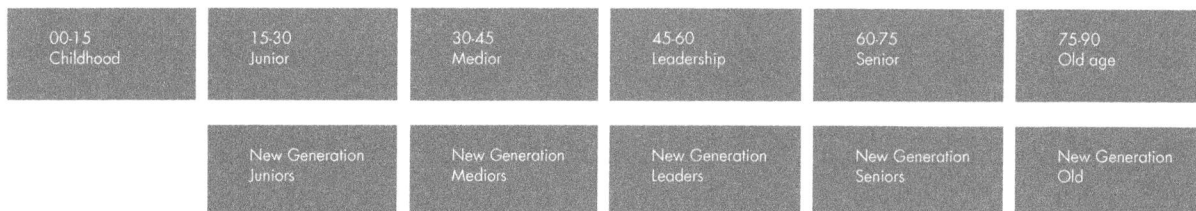

00-15 Childhood	15-30 Junior	30-45 Medior	45-60 Leadership	60-75 Senior	75-90 Old age
	New Generation Juniors	New Generation Mediors	New Generation Leaders	New Generation Seniors	New Generation Old

Fig. 1 Dutch generations entering (2015) their next life phase

From the Silent Generation (1925-1940) arose the Connecting Generation X (1955-1970) in the Netherlands. The Silent Generation had a rather closed attitude, was not open in dealing with their emotions and was oriented towards authority when it came to questions such as what is good or what is bad. The X parents have very open communication with their Y children, and they encourage their children to be authentic. When Dutch Y children ask questions about what is good or bad, their parents say things like: "What do you think yourself. I have some suggestions but you have to figure it out for yourself." These are just some examples of fundamental changes in the area of social behavior that bring forward new social patterns, which are created in the early interaction between parents and their children.

Fig. 2 A new generation of parents

Be ready for a surprise. My generation research in the Netherlands shows that new social patterns spring from the contemporary interaction between parents and their children. The seeds for the updates brought by a new generation are sown in young families; the new culture patterns are born there. The source of new patterns that are an important part of the foundation of a new generation is found in differences between the parenting style of a new generation of parents and the way these parents were raised by their parents (fig.2). The foundation of a new young generation is solidified at the end of their first life stage (see fig. 1).

Moreover, children seem to provoke a contemporary way of upbringing, because of their hypersensitivity towards outdated patterns. Many parents reported resistance by their children when they accidentally acted in an old-fashioned way, i.e. when some of their parenting patterns were out of date.

Fresh patterns form the characteristics of a generation and are at the same time potential updates for the surrounding culture. After childhood, a generation becomes aware of their characteristics that differ from the older generations. Their power to update the surrounding culture that was built by former generations increases with every life stage, up until the phase of leadership. During the phase of seniorhood, the impact on the surrounding culture decreases.

Life experience and professional expertise make seniors very suitable to support juniors in their development and in their updating efforts.

The number of vital Dutch seniors who want to keep working beyond their retirement age is growing. To be better able to work together with younger generations, seniors have to let go of and update some of their deep-rooted routines that are past their expiration date. I will go into this process in Chapter 4.

Successive generations form continually moving horizontal layers in every (organizational) culture. This is visualized in fig. 3. Each new generation, from the oldest in their life stage to the youngest one in their life stage, has the potency to replace outdated patterns by new ones. These culture-updating processes can be supported, slowed down or blocked, unconsciously or consciously, willingly or unwillingly. With awareness, more care and supporting actions, these processes can be improved.

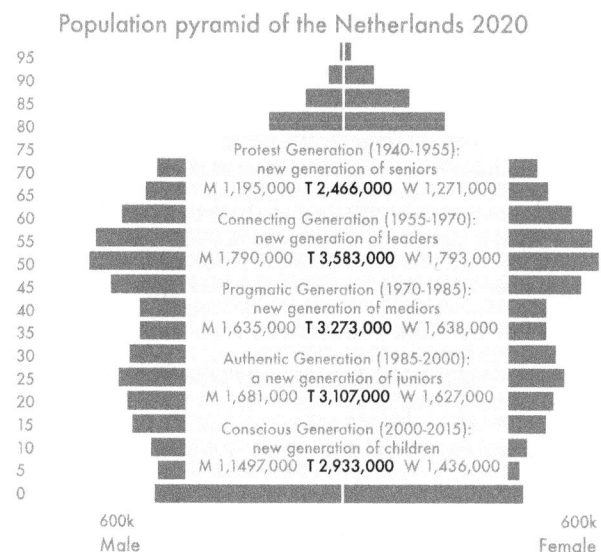

Population pyramid of the Netherlands 2020

Protest Generation (1940-1955):
new generation of seniors
M 1,195,000 T 2,466,000 W 1,271,000

Connecting Generation (1955-1970):
new generation of leaders
M 1,790,000 T 3,583,000 W 1,793,000

Pragmatic Generation (1970-1985):
new generation of mediors
M 1,635,000 T 3.273,000 W 1,638,000

Authentic Generation (1985-2000):
a new generation of juniors
M 1,681,000 T 3,107,000 W 1,627,000

Conscious Generation (2000-2015):
new generation of children
M 1,1497,000 T 2,933,000 W 1,436,000

600k
Male

600k
Female

Fig. 3 The successive generations as layers in their (Dutch) culture

Members of all generations suffer from energy loss when they repeat outdated social patterns. The younger generation is most sensitive to these outdated routines.

Older generations have the tendency to repeat outdated patterns, despite the fact that this drains their energy. Not because they want to, but because it is autopilot behavior. To get an idea of what I mean here, think about how you are used to driving on the right or left side of the road. For instance, when you are used to driving on the right side of the road in your country – which is a deep-rooted habit – and you go to England, you know that you have to drive on the left, to survive in traffic. The tendency to drive on the right can be strong, even when you know that this is dangerous. The more complex the traffic situation is, the sooner this deep-rooted tendency might come forward automatically. In social and economic life, repetition of outdated patterns is dangerous for the same reason. It will lead, sooner or later, quickly or slowly, to the social and economic death of your (working) community.

When juniors are overrun by outdated patterns, their reaction can be intense. In the worst case, members of the youngest generation develop apathy or aggression. When tension between the younger and the older generation is high, the aggression of the youngsters is often expressed towards leaders or institutions that are seen as symbols of the old culture. This can lead to social explosions. When their trust in any change is low, youngsters might leave their group and community, or their aggression and frustration might turn inward and lead to depression and destructive behavior, such as alcohol or drug abuse.

The youngest working generation at companies and other institutions can be compared to what the canary birds did for miners. Miners took canaries into the mines with them, because canaries are very sensitive to air pollution. Whenever pollution levels came close to the point of being life threatening for the miners, the canaries would fall off their branches and the miners would run away to find healthy air. These canaries saved many lives in the mines, thanks to their sensitivity to air pollution and thanks to the attention of the miners themselves. Canary birds' response to polluted air can be compared to the youngest generations' energy response at their organizations, as warning signs of the organization's social, economic and ecological health.

Around 1993, I noticed in the Netherlands for the first time that many young professionals at the beginning of their professional life, which at that time were juniors from the Pragmatic Generation (1970-1985), were losing their freshness and their work energy – often within a couple of minutes – after they got involved in projects with many outdated patterns. These observations formed the foundation for my generation research. Through these juniors, I discovered what caused the loss of energy and freshness, and which interventions were effective in countering this.

Aging Dutch and other European companies

Most Dutch and other European companies and institutions are aging. In fig. 4, you can find more details about population aging in Europe. The major risk of an aging workforce for organizations is the repetition of social patterns that are outdated. This repetition is not only a major drain on employees' energy, it is also economically life threatening for those (work) communities. Nevertheless, aging can offer great possibilities as well. The oldest generations are the largest. There have never been so many seniors with so much work experience across Dutch and other European organizations. Making the most of the rich expertise and life experience of older generations, combined with support for the freshness and evolutionary value of the smaller younger generations, is becoming one of the biggest challenges for old economies in surviving in the decades to come.

Never before were so many experienced seniors participating in the (work) community in the Netherlands and other European aging countries as today. The contribution of seniors to society will keep on rising over the coming decades and their labor participation will increase. At the same time, smaller generations of young people will enter the labor market. These facts combined will lead to aging workforces at organizations and other institutions, all over Europe. It is expected that this phenomenon will peak around 2035 and that it will slowly fade away from that time onwards.

Worldwide, average life expectancy has increased from 48 to 68 years over the past 55 years. This is a rise of about four months per year, two and a half days per week and eight hours per day. This spectacular rise is likely to continue in the future. In Europe and many other developed parts of the world, increasing life expectancy is accompanied by declining in birth rates. The average European woman gives birth to one and a half child, which is rather less than the replacement level. These two developments are the reason why Europe is the continent that suffers most from the phenomenon of population aging. The speed of population aging will decrease gradually. Germany, Italy, Greece and Sweden belong to the fastest aging countries in Europe. While the population in the Netherlands is relatively young at this point, population aging will substantially increase over the coming twenty-five years. Average life expectancy in the Netherlands has increased to 80.5 (in 1860, this was 37 years). The average number of children per woman was approximately 1.6 in 2013 (around 1900, this was 4.5). As a matter of fact, there are many regional differences when it comes to the degree to which organizations are aging in the Netherlands. In (expensive) commuter towns and in regions where the population is shrinking (the province of Zeeland, the southern part of the province of Limburg, and parts of the north and east of the Netherlands), the population is relatively old. In the west of the country, in the large cities and the first overspill towns, the population is aging far less swiftly.

Source: the Dutch Interdisciplinary demographic institute (Nederlands Interdisciplinair Demografisch Instituut), "Bevolkingsvraagstukken in Nederland anno 2012"

Fig. 4 Aging in the Netherlands and Europe

For several reasons, many employees and managers seem to overlook the fact that within their organization, autonomous natural forces are at work. A strong focus on top-level managers and on rational reasoning when it comes to organizational change might be one of the reasons. A strong focus on making money in the short run might be another one. As early as in the 1980s, management guru Henry Mintzberg warned managers at bigger companies about the negative effect of the dominance of rational management: 'It seemed that managers lost their intuition skills ...' The evolutionary powers of successive generations are not seen at most companies. 'If you cannot see it, you cannot use it,' is a saying coined by the best Dutch football player in history, Johan Cruyff. Cruyff and Mintzberg might be on to something.

My research – based on scientific work by Marías Aguilera, Ortega y Gasset, Mannheim, Strauss and Howe and Becker – provides evidence of the overlooked natural and evolutionary change potency of successive generations. Each generation is geared by birth to update the social system to which they belong. Let us call it the destiny or instincts of a generation, through which a generation tries to increase the chance of survival of their own social system, group and community.

At most (aging) organizations in the Netherlands, these natural forces are, involuntarily and subconsciously, more often inhibited than supported. Is this a bad thing? Yes, this is a very bad thing. It allows a social, economic and ecological disaster to slowly creep in. Talent and vital survival power drains away or even disappears, the culture becomes outdated, all livelihood slowly disappears, followed by economic death. Some people call it creative destruction, but I call it a mistake in our culture or a missed opportunity.

Strong tendency to repeat outdated patterns

The tendency to subconsciously repeat outdated social

patterns can be very strong. For the moment, I would like to point out six causes of this tendency, which I found at many Dutch organizations:

1 Many organizations grew strong during the second half of the last century, under the leadership of the Protest Generation (1940-1955). Within these organizations, many social patterns persist that were developed by the Protest Generation and their focus on democratizing, such as ways of gathering and decision making, ways of communication and organizing. However, 01/01/2000 was the expiration date of many of these patterns that created the social economic success at the end of the last century. From that day onwards, these outdated patterns started to drain away work energy.

2 Members of older generations have a strong tendency to subconsciously repeat these quite deep-rooted outdated patterns, despite the fact that these patterns drain away their own work energy as well. Energy loss slowly creeps in and is hard to notice. These seniors are like fish in the water who are unaware of the pollution that is creeping in.

3 More than 80 % of Dutch organizations will keep aging as time passes, until 2035. Over the next decades, the older working generation will be the biggest and the younger the smallest. That means that an increasing number of people will be people who tend to repeat outdated patterns.

4 Within many organizations, the Connecting Generation X (1955-1970) and the Pragmatic Generation (1970-1985) have failed to renew a number of outdated patterns. Instead, they have adapted to these patterns involuntarily and mostly subconsciously. Therefore, these patterns have started to become a deeper-rooted part of the culture. This makes it even more difficult to change these habits.

5 The ability of the youngest working generation to update their culture is often overrated. To really do their updating work, these juniors need the assistance and active support of experienced colleagues from the bigger and older gene-rations. This support is only scarcely offered or not offered at all, and juniors generally do not ask for it either. This is not because seniors refuse to ask for it, but rather because they are often not aware of the meaning of energy loss at work – stagnation in social evolution – or do not see it or do not know what to do, when they see it.

6 The ability of the youngest working generation to scan outdated patterns is not estimated at its true value and remains, in this way, unutilized. A 'culture MRI scan' performed by the smallest and youngest working generation is usually crystal clear. It shows the outdated patterns and the updates by the youngest working generation while also providing insight into the speed of the actual culture evolution. However, many professionals are still looking to the top of the hierarchy when it comes to what needs to be done. Many top-level managers are more focused on analyses by consultancy firms.

This book answers the question of how generations that succeed each other in life stages, from the oldest to the youngest generation, can exert or rediscover their power to stimulate the social evolution from within the professional heart of 'their' organization (culture).
To understand the evolutionary potency of successive generations, it is important to understand the essence of the generation perspective. In the next chapter, I will show how I developed a generation theory, building on work by other scientists. I have done my best to write it in an accessible way, but if you do not like theories, you could decide to just read the last two pages of the next chapter. This will improve your understanding of the phenomenon of generations and of what I wrote about the culture updates of the Dutch working generations.

On reflexes, free will and responsibility

Victor Lamme (2010) uses many examples to show us that we are often controlled by habits that have left deep traces in our mind. Based on this hypothesis, he wonders whether human beings even possess free will at all. Lamme: "Everything we go through, consciously or subconsciously, leaves traces in the neural pathways of our brain that run between stimulus and response. These traces strengthen certain neural pathways and weaken others. In the end, our history determines what we decide when we have to choose from multiple alternatives. These stimulus-outcome couplings exist from the day on which we are born and they strengthen or weaken the neural pathways in our brain. At a given moment, our brain, that -until this point- had only been armed with preferences that were mostly determined genetically and by upbringing style, makes its own 'decision'. A child takes its first steps and 'chooses' to go either left or right. The child falls down on its nose or down the staircase. Most choices involve either positive or negative consequences. Reward or punishment; pleasure or pain. In this way, couplings between stimulus and behavior are being trained in a Pavlovian way. Every decision inevitably leads to a history that is unique for every individual, until the next dilemma presents itself.

"Intelligent reflexes such as top sport performances require long-term training. For most sports, athletes need to train the coordination between their eyes and their hand or foot. These couplings need to be drilled into the neural pathways of our brain that need to convert sensorial information into behavior. It is a type of sensorial-motoric learning, which requires much repetition. Everything you repeat gets drilled into your brain. For some reason – that remains unclear to this day – this process requires a good night's rest. Patterns seem to repeat themselves during the night and will not be truly drilled into your brain until the next morning."

"Every member of society is exposed to more or less the same experiences via the existing culture, which means that every brain contains a standard repertoire of automatisms and reflexes, such as driving a car, eating, learning and reading. Individual automatisms exist as well, like the way in which someone holds a pen, walks or smiles. During the day, we effortlessly switch from one automatism to the other. The perception of the existence of an 'I' that decides what we do, is more than just an illusion. It is a complete misconception. Many people feel uncomfortable with the idea that they do not control their behavior with their ratio and thoughts, but only commentate on it. Are we not responsible for our own deeds? Yes, of course we are. We determine our own unique history by deciding what we should (not) do. Not by what we say. That brain history is impossible to reconstruct. What we do see is the result of this history in the present."

Fig. 5 Victor Lamme on free will and autopilot behavior

2 Towards a generational theory

Early thinking about generations

Over the course of the past two centuries, several famous historians, sociologists and philosophers have provided different components that have helped me develop a generational theory.

In 1803, French historian Jean-Louis Giraud-Soulavie (1753-1813) described generations as groups that succeed each other 'in power and control' every fifteen years. He based this description on detailed studies of influential people and important events in the eighteenth century. In 1839, French philosopher and founder of sociology Auguste Comte wrote that social progress depends on a continuing shift of changers. One certain generation makes way for the following generation. The evolutionary pace springs from 'the struggle' between the 'instincts' of preservation, which is typically seen in older people, and the 'instincts' of innovation, which is typically seen in young people. In 1893, French sociologist Émile Durkheim noted that social change is restricted whenever a particular generation is strongly influenced by the older generation. Social change gains speed as soon as the generational group is larger and dissolute. This happens, for example, in big cities with a young population. These cities attract many young people from elsewhere. These juniors have succeeded to withdraw themselves from the traditions according to which they were brought up. Around 1875, German historian, sociologist and philosopher Wilhelm Dilthey wrote that

1 One generation covers a certain period of time, which starts at birth and ends when a new generation appears.

2 Members of the same generation feel related to each other because they grow up with each other and they are all subject to the same guiding influences during their formative years.

Fig. 6 An overview of what European scientists wrote about generations in the 19th century

Year	Source	Essence
1809	Jean-Louis Giraud-Soulavie, Pièces inédites sur les règnes de Louis XIV, Louis XV et Louis XVI	Generations are human groupings that succeed each other in power and control every fifteen years.
1824	Leopold von Ranke, Geschichte der Romanischen und Germanischen Völker im 15. und 16. Jahrhundert	It would perhaps be a worthy task to present generations one after the other, as they are bound to each other and as they separate on the stage of universal history. One might describe a series of illustrious figures, those men who in every generation maintain close relationships and whose antagonisms advance the world's evolution. Events correspond to the nature of such men.
1839	Auguste Comte, Cours de philosophie positive	Our social progress is essentially dependent on the continual and sufficiently rapid renewal of the agents of general change, if one generation gives way to the following. But our social evolution is incompatible with either an excessively slow or an overly rapid renovation of human generations.
1843	John Stuart Mill: A System of Logic, Ratiocinative and Inductive	The proximate cause of every state of society is the state immediately preceding it. Society is understood as a series of successive situations. The periods which most distinctly mark these successive changes being intervals of one generation, during which a new set of human beings have been educated, have grown up from childhood and taken possession of society.

1854	Leoplold von Ranke, Über die Epochen der neueren Geschichte. Vorträge dem Könige Maxmilian II von Bayern gehalten, Weltgeschichte IV (1910)	Progress consists in the fact that in each successive period human life potential increases, and hence that each generation completely outstrips those preceding it, and that the last would always be the most privileged, while those preceding would be merely the foundation of those following... But this I affirm: every period is immediate to God, and its worth springs from its very existence... I believe that in any generation real moral greatness is the same as in any other... there is no superior power.
1861	Justin Dromel, La loi des révolutions.	There are two fully active groups engaged in a great political debate, those who struggle to gain power (from age > 25, those who have power but are gradually losing it (age < 65). The individual and his entire generation have certain inflexibility, in the sense that they remain faithful to their own principles.
1872	Antoine Cournot, Considérations sur la marche des idées et des événements dans les temps modernes.	Each generation transmits to the one immediately following a certain wealth of ideas through education; the educating generation is still influenced by all the survivors of a previous generation. The observation of historical facts can accurately show us how the gradual renovation of ideas results from the imperceptible replacement of older generations by the younger, and how much time is necessary for change.
1874	Giuseppe Ferrari, Teoria dei periodi politici.	The political generation is composed of men who are born, who live and die in the same years, and who, whether friends or enemies, belong to the same society. These generations assume different historical roles in a larger drama that lasts 125 years. Each principle needs four generations or acts to complete its total evolution and bring its circle to a close. The first generation of a period is preliminary or preparatory, the second revolutionary or explosive, the third is reactionary, and the fourth is harmonizing.
1875	Gustav Rümelin, Reden und Aufsätze; über den Begriff und die dauer einer Generation.	It is not violent revolutions that transform human life in periodic thrusts; rather the small difference between parents and children in customs and ways of looking at things are generalized to a point of mass effect, shaping cultural history of mankind.
1875	Wilhelm Dilthey, Über das Studium der Geschichte der Wissenschaften vom Menschen, der Gesellschaft und dem Stat, in Philosophische Montashefte.	An inner measure of psychic time corresponds to the seconds and minutes of a clock; 'human life' and the progression of its 'ages' correspond to the decades and centuries of historical movement. A generation is a span of time, an inner metrical notion of human life. A generation is also a term applied to a relationship of contemporaneity between individuals, between those who grew up together, who had a common childhood, a common adolescence, whose years of greatest manly vigor partially overlap. A generation is composed of a tightly bound circle of individuals who are linked as to form a unit made homogeneous by dependence on the same great events and variations that appeared in their formative age, whatever the diversity of other additional factors.
1881	Louis Benloew, Les Lois de l'histoire.	France, from 1515-1700, had twelve evolutions with a mean of fifteen years and five months; England, from 1625-1760, had nine evolutions, with a mean of fifteen years; Greece, from 510- 301 BC, had nineteen evolutions with a mean of fifteen years.
1886	Ottokar Lorenz, Die Geschichtswissenschaft in Hauptrichtungen und Aufgaben kritisch erörtert.	In the course of a century, there are three generations linked in a true relationship, transmitting their experiences directly to each other, and thus constituting a spiritual, historical unity. Historical evolution is based then on the real succession of generations.
1893	Émile Durkheim, De la division du travail social.	Social change is limited and slow when a generation is strongly subjected to the influence of tradition and the old, and accelerated when groupings are larger and men less bound.

The Hungarian-German sociologist Karl Mannheim (1893-1947) is widely considered the founder of generational thinking. This is not completely true. José Ortega y Gasset (1883-1955), a Spanish philosopher and a contemporary of Mannheim's, had some interesting thoughts about generations and the masses, but hesitated to publish his ideas. His younger colleague Julián Marías Aguilera (1914-2005) collected Ortega's ideas about generations, as well as those of other early thinkers (fig. 6) and was the first to try to develop a generational theory. Julián Marías was a student of Ortega's and later became a friend and colleague.

In 1928, Mannheim published a number of comprehensive basic principles. One of these principles implied the idea that generations form social layers within a culture, which are based on time of birth and biological rhythm. People who are born in the same period and share the same perception of a surrounding 'zeitgeist' develop a connection with their peers. These peers also share a similar physical, mental and psychological development and a certain destiny in life. This is what he calls the 'entelechy' of a generation: the unique combination of one's own nature, a shared collective development and a shared reaction to outdated patterns in the dominating spirit of the age. Thanks to the constant introduction of new generations that carry their unique 'entelechy', the culture is undergoing a continual transformation. On the interface of childhood and adolescence, a generation becomes aware of what they wish to change in their culture. All aspects of a surrounding culture that members of a young generation do not experience as problematic are automatically and subconsciously assimilated by them.

According to Julián Marías, around 1923 his colleague and friend José Ortega y Gasset (1883-1995) was the first to formulate a theory that could be labeled as a beginning of a generational theory. It originated from Ortega's theory on social and historical reality, which was more general. Ortega's thoughts on social and historical reality can be summarized as follows:

1 About people as individuals:
   • Reality is neither 'I', nor 'things'. Reality is life itself. My life is a sum of what I do with my own possibilities and limitations and the possibilities and limitations of the given circumstances.
   • Life has been given to me as an inevitable task. It is not perfect. It is up to me to make life perfect, to decide what to do and not to do in order to achieve this. That is why I need an image or a notion of the direction in which I need to go.
   • Man is inevitably free. The only freedom of which man does not dispose is the freedom to stop being free.

2 About people in their social environment:
   • Every one of us lives in a world full of systems with stubborn habits and conventions with shared interpretations of reality.
   • The world is not perfect; it copes with many gaps and problems. People are continuingly (re)forming the world. They turn the world into their own 'home'.
   • The most important sources for change in the social world consist of primary feelings (vital sensitivity) towards the existing life. Some feelings and changes are superficial and others are more profound.
   • We can distinguish two types of changes: changes *in* the existing world and changes *of* the existing world.
   • The mass is susceptible to influence exercised by outstandingly energetic people.

3 About the individual and his or her generation.
   • Changes that are brought about by vital sensitivity that changes the world itself appear in the shape of generations. A generation itself is a radical social change. Individuals are able to bring about changes in the world. Generations are able to bring about changes of the world and this

is how they form the pivot of our historical evolution.

• Every generation has a small group of energetic people with a well-developed vital sensitivity who form characterizing figures in their own generation. They form the vanguard of their generation. This group influences its environment strongly.

• Without new generations emerging, history would suddenly stop evolving. It would no longer be possible to prime any form of radical social innovation whatsoever.

• Every generation has a two-dimensional task in life: receiving as well as taking over everything the previous generation left them and expressing its own spontaneous impulses of renewal.

• At a certain historical moment, two different generations are most actively participating in society. The generation that has members between the ages of 30 to 45 years old, and the generation that has members between the ages of 45 to 60 years old.

Julián Marías Aguilera was the first to thoroughly study early written works on generations. He also clarified the brainwork of Ortega y Gasset. In 1967, his work *El método histórico de las generaciones* was published, which was translated into English in 1970. Marías developed a method to localize generations. According to him, this requires knowledge of the system of dominating habits. This system adds structure to life at a certain moment in history and it surpasses individual life. It thrusts itself on life and conditions it. According to Marías, the act of localizing generations requires knowledge about the surrounding culture and about the beginning of historical innovations. After every generational shift, a new system of new dominating conventions arises. Marías interpreted this new system as a new lifestyle, which is clearly different from the old one, a new way of living. Just like democracy in the nineteenth century or rationalism in the seventeenth century. Such an innova-

tion takes place within the entire society. Historical innovation concerns every generation; some historical innovations require that more generations than just one make an effort to contribute to it. The bounds between generations can be found in portraying the vanguard of a generation and their dominating habits and in analyzing the variation that exists within those habits.

Marías pictured generations as mountain chains in a landscape (fig. 7). The area between the mountain chains forms the borderline. The mountain slopes represent years of birth. It is possible for two spots on a slope that are far away from each other to still lie on the same mountain. Whereas two spots that are close to each other can lie on two separate mountains. Every person finds himself in a certain spot in his or her own generation: at the beginning, in the middle or at the end.

Ortega y Gasset and Marías mentioned energetic people that are the vanguard of a generation. Generation research in the Netherlands (Diepstraten et al. 1999; SCP, 2010) showed that about 15 % of the people in a generation said that they do not experience a (close) connection to their generation. This has led us to believe that there might be a group of informal leaders in every generation of about 15 %, a group of followers of about 70 % and a group of unconnected members of about 15 % (fig. 7).

Marías also worked out the idea of life stages (fig. 2 and fig. 9): every life consists of five stages of fifteen years each, starting with childhood and ending with old age. With every life stage a person goes through, the amount of influence their generation has on society increases. In the fourth stage, between the 45th and 60th year of life, a generation has the biggest influence on the surrounding culture. After a generation has reached this age, its influence decreases. The influence that remains from the senior life phase will consist of passing (working) life experience on to younger

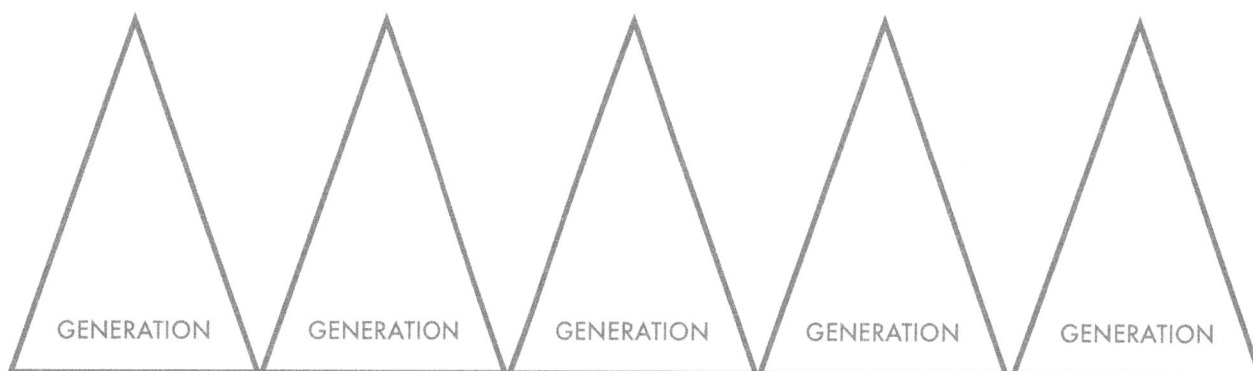

GENERATION   GENERATION   GENERATION   GENERATION   GENERATION

Followers within generations (± 70%):
are less energetic and expressive and do not show clearly the characteristics of their generation. By doing so they have lesser influence on their (working) environment. They might influence it indirectly, namely by supporting the informal leaders of their generation.

Not connected to their own generation (± 15 %)
About 15% of the population feels less (or not at all) connected to their own generation and does not experience to be of any influence on the surrounding (organizational) culture.

Fig. 7 Generations, with leaders and followers, displayed as mountain chains in a landscape

generations and to coach juniors to find their own way in (working) life.

The founders of generational thinking are from France, Spain and Germany. However, the lion's share of research that has been done on generations was published in the United States and the Netherlands in the second half of the twentieth century. Many – more recent – publications are about the youngest generation. Authors have used many different dates of birth and names for this generation: Generation Y, Millennials, Screenagers, the Internet Generation, the Boundless Generation, the Authentic Generation Y. Only a few publications are about all generations. It is very hard to find well-founded scientific research on generations. In the U.S., Strauss and Howe tried to come to a generation classification in a more or less scientific way.

Marías philosophized profoundly and developed a method enabling the localization of generations, but he did not apply his method himself. American researchers William Strauss and Neil Howe did employ this method in a way. In 1991, they localized generations in American history in their study called Generations, The History of America's Future, 1584 to 2069. This large-scale study of American history builds on the substantial method of Marías. For unclear reasons, they used life stages that spanned 22 years in 1991, and 20 years in 1998. By using these time spans, Strauss and Howe deviate from one of Marías' substantial principles: the biological rhythm of generations, which states that a generational shift takes place every fifteen years. There is a good chance that Strauss and Howe's generational classification is incorrect. Their most important contribution to the development of a generational theory consists of their elaboration of the insight that generations succeed each other in life stages. They studied this more thoroughly than Marías had. The time span of a generation – a cluster of years of birth – equals the time span of a life stage – a cluster of years of age. In every stage of life, a generation has a different function in society. The function of members of a generation during their years of youth differs from their function in the leadership stage or the senior stage. Every generation has its 'peer personality' with strengths and weaknesses that characterize that particular generation. That is why every successive generation shapes life in a certain stage of life differently from its predecessor, according to Strauss and Howe. They also introduced the concept of a 'generational constellation': all present generations combined form a certain constellation; an interactive and unique combination, which characterizes the spirit of the age. Every time a generation succeeds the previous one, this does not only mean that every generation enters the next life stage, it also means that the constellation changes. This generation shift produces two types of consequences:

1 The effect of the new generation in the (next) life stage. The successive generation lives its life in this stage differently from the previous one.

2 The effect of the new generational constellation, where the influence of the oldest generation ebbs away, and where the youngest generation's influence on their surrounding community and its institutions increases. This changes the interaction between generations and the spirit of the age in that community substantially.

These changes in society (and its social systems) surface a couple of years after a generational shift took place. Only in a 'free' society, the impact of a generation on the surrounding culture can be fully established. In a society where people do not experience freedom to express themselves openly, for example in societies in which leaders from the oldest generation impose their beliefs on the younger generations, it is very difficult to accomplish this, if not downright impossible. Open interaction between generations speeds up the evolutionary process. Minimized interaction or a closed relationship between generations or the domination of one generation will slow down or even block social-evolutionary processes.

In 2000, Zemke, Raines and Filipczak came up with a description of 'generations at work'. They addressed the question of how to prevent generational conflicts and how to optimize collaboration between generations. The gist of their findings is the following: it is important for generations to become aware of the differences between their own generation and generations above and below them, and to keep these differences in mind during the process of developing a suited HR policy and in collaboration processes. The three scientists based their findings on case studies of five companies in which generations work together in harmony, as well as on interviews they held with experts. Although they did employ the generational classifications of Strauss and Howe, they did not go into the evolutionary function of generations.

In the early 1990s, Dutch professor and sociologist Henk Becker of Utrecht University was the first to carry out a sociological study of generations in the Netherlands. He based his study on Mannheim's work and he used trend breaks – for instance wars and economic crises – as a basic principle for the localization of generations. His focus was on the impact of the actual spirit of the age on (young) generations in society. In his work *Generaties en hun kansen* (Generations and their opportunities) (1992), Becker identified the emergence of five generations, until the Pragmatic Generation. According to him, this classification counts for Western Europe.

In 1999, Diepstraten, Esther and Vinken profoundly studied the validity of Becker's generational classification. Well over three-quarters of the Dutch population recognized themselves as members of a generation that conformed to Becker's classification. We could take this to mean that the remaining quarter of the Dutch population does not display any generation-characterizing behavior. I did find two variations: some people do not feel any connection with their generation and some people feel connected with all generations. According to the study by Diepstraten et al., this quarter does not experience being of any influence on their environment. The remaining three-quarters of Dutch citizens do feel like they influence their environment. The researchers concluded that the Dutch population has a rather large generational consciousness.

In 1991, Van Berkel, Van Schaik and Snippenburg studied Henk Becker's generational classification. Van den Broek studied this classification in 2001. They were able to conclude that generational differences do not occur in 'all areas' and that perhaps a generation is formed in a different way than Becker stated.

My research of two generations of parents and of the generation of their children showed that it is highly probable that the foundation of a new generation (of children) can be found in changes in upbringing. Changes are caused by differences between the ways the parents were brought up by their parents, for instance with no sharing of emotions and a focus on authority, and the way they bring up their children, for instance openly sharing emotions and a focus on authenticity. Trend breaks in society and historical events, such as wars or crises, might influence the way parents bring up their children. The seeds of new culture patterns in the Netherlands are probably sown by young

Dutch families. The new social patterns are shaped in the interaction between children and their parents and become a characteristic part of children's lives around the age of twelve. These pre-research findings might be an interesting field for future research.

Every two years, the Netherlands Institute for Social Research publishes a socio-cultural report. In 2010, this report was entitled '*Wisseling van de wacht: generaties in Nederland*' (Changing of the guard: generations in the Netherlands). It remains a mystery why the institute chose this title. Perhaps, they chose it because there was (and still is) much public attention for this phenomenon. The report, which numbers 563 pages, is – unfortunately enough – not about generations. The report mentions an analytical knot that made it impossible to carry out good generation research. This knot can be explained in three questions. First: are differences between generations the effect of being born in the same period of time (is it a cohort effect)? Second: are characteristics of a generation the effect of being in a certain life phase (effect of their age)? Third: are differences between generations the effect of differences in the spirit of the age in their formative years? This knot remains untied in their report.

I did unravel the knot by focusing my research on the following questions:

A What are the differences between the former and the successive generation in the same life stage (in the same age group)?

B What is the reaction of a generation in their life phase to the surrounding culture (to the actual spirit of the age) in terms of updates in the culture that was built by former generations?

The outcomes of A and B are the same. The differences between the former and the new generation in a life phase are the updates by a new generation. These updates by a generation can be found in the area that generates most of their energy (at work). Their reaction to the outdated culture patterns can be found in the area that is their biggest energy drain at work.

The most important reason to start my generational research was the fact that around 1993 I observed at different organizations a quick loss of fresh views and work energy within the first cohorts of the Pragmatic Generation (1970-1985), shortly after they started their working life. In 1995, I met the Dutch scientist who imported the generation perspective into the Netherlands, Henk Becker, by chance. Our conversations have helped me to understand that my observations had something to do with a young generation that is confronted with an organizational culture that was built by previous generations. Juniors in that time often said that they felt thwarted by older colleagues. 'We want to renew and innovate, but our older colleagues do not support us, they do not want to change anything.' However, these juniors never verified this assumption. I have researched this assumption many times. I did not find a lack of will, but I discovered that unconscious repetition of deep-rooted and outdated routines by seniors created a frustrating wall for juniors. From another viewpoint you can say that juniors' interpretation of seniors' behavior created the wall or at least strengthened the wall. Along the way, I started doing experiments using interventions. The most important intervention was to stimulate, in different ways, the youngest working generation to keep doing those things at work that energized them, and do them mindfully. As I continued my research, I searched for ways to enable members of the youngest generations to innovate the existing culture. Later on, I searched for ways to enable all new working generations to do so in their next life phase.

During the first ten years of my experimental research, no one was interested in the results. My curiosity and fascination kept on increasing. Around the year 2000, I decided to do my doctoral research on how generations within organi-

zations play their role in the evolution of the culture of their organization. I was particularly interested in the ways in which generations that succeed each other in life stages influence the development of organizational cultures and how this natural process of culture evolution could be supported. A literature review showed me that a coherent generational theory did not yet exist. This may have been the reason why no one in the world had ever done any research on how generations function within organizations. A different explanation could have been the fact that there was no appropriate research method available. In the appendix, I will describe the generation research methodology that I developed and that I tested in the Netherlands and in Brazil.

I created a generation theory by connecting all scientific fragments about generations from Marías Aguilera, Ortega y Gasset, Mannheim, Strauss and Howe and Becker. I then added my own findings. The most important principles of this theory are:

1 A generation consists of 15 birth cohorts (consecutive years of birth) of contemporaries who are connected by:
   • A shared upbringing and a shared perception of the vitality of the surrounding culture,
   • A shared reaction expressed by spontaneous impulses of renewing outdated patterns,
   • A shared mental, emotional and physical development, attuned to the evolutionary function of their generation

1A The characteristics of a generation are solidified in the first twelve years. They are shaped in the interaction between parents and their children, and the result of differences in the way the parents were brought up and the way these parents bring up their children.

2 The difference between one generation and the previous generation in a particular life stage forms the source for the renewal of outdated cultural patterns. This evolutionary potency can also be found in the area that gains most of their energy at work.

3　Social patterns that generate most energy in a generation show the direction of the social evolution of the culture that they are part of. Every generation has a vanguard, consisting of the most energetic people of that particular generation. This group has the biggest influence on the working environment and characterizes its generation the most.

4　Outdated social patterns can be found in the area that is a drain on energy (at work) in all (working) generations, from the youngest to the oldest one. The youngest (working) generation is the most sensitive to outdated patterns.

5　The intensity and quality of the interaction between generations in a culture determine the speed of social evolution. A generation cannot fulfill its evolutionary function if other generations – for whatever reason – are not open to their impulses of renewal. Active support by the other generations accelerates the process of social evolution.

6　Social patterns from preceding generations that are still vital are automatically taken over by new generations.

7　Every fifteen years – in the Netherlands in 2000, 2015, 2030 etcetera – a generation shift starts. In that year, the first cohort of a generation enters their next life phase. Fifteen years later, the last cohort enters that same life phase. Depending on the quality and intensity of interaction between the generations in a culture, the effects of the generation shift become visible halfway through the shift.

Generations that succeed each other in life stages shape new generations of seniors, leaders, mediors and juniors that react spontaneously to the vitality of the surrounding culture by a focus on revitalizing outdated social patterns. This process of culture evolution keeps the social system – society, organizations, associations, political parties and the like – of which they are part themselves, up to date.

Fig. 8 Research about the opposite of culture evolution: culture destruction

Good people and evil behavior

This book is about constructive behavior and evolution of cultures, but people can also behave destructively and do the opposite of what needs to be done to contribute to the evolution of the culture of their community. Two experiments show what can (also) happen.

Philip George Zimbardo (1933) is a psychologist and a professor emeritus at Stanford University. He became known for his 1971 Stanford prison experiment. In this experiment, 24 clinically sane individuals were randomly assigned to be "prisoners" or "guards" in a mock dungeon located in the basement of the psychology building at Stanford. The volunteers knew they were being used in a study but they did not know when the study would be taking place, so the initial action of being randomly arrested one morning and taken to the mock prison put them in a mild state of shock. On arrival, the "prisoners" were stripped, searched, shaved and deloused, which caused a great deal of humiliation. They were then issued uniforms, ID numbers, and escorted to their cells by the volunteer prison guards. The guards themselves were not given any specific instruction or guidelines for the way they were to treat the prisoners besides the fact they were not allowed to use corporal punishment. Instead, the psychologists allowed them to do whatever was needed to keep order in the prison. They were dressed in identical uniforms, wore a whistle around their neck and carried a nightstick.

At the beginning, the volunteer prisoners did not take the guards and their authority seriously. The prisoners mocked the guards, trying to regain their individuality. This, however, was short-lived. The prisoners soon realized that the attitude of the guards was very serious and that they demanded obedience. This began a long string of confrontational quarrels between the guards and prisoners. The guards used physical punishment and exercises, such as pushups, in order to show their authority to the prisoners.

In the morning of only the second day, a rebellion broke out among the volunteer prisoners. They ripped off their uniforms and locked themselves in their cells by pushing their beds up against the door. In response to this, the guards became very angry and called for backup. Guards who were not on duty were called in and the guards who were assigned to only the night shift stayed with the guards who came in all the way through their shift the next morning. The tactic the guards came up with was to fight back in order to discipline the unruly prisoners and make them obey. In response to the prisoners barricading themselves in their cells, the guards used fire extinguishers on them to get them away from the entrances. Once the guards were able to get into the cells, they stripped the inmates naked, tore apart the beds and the cell, and put the prisoners who had started the rebellion in solitary confinement.

On the third day, the study allowed visiting hours for friends and family. The visitation was closely monitored and timed with many rules and restrictions. The next event that added to the prison experiment "drama" was a rumored escape plan that the prisoners were planning on carrying out directly after visiting hours. The prisoner was going to have some of his friends round up, break into the prison and free all of the prisoners. After one of the guards overheard this plan, an informant was placed in among the prisoners and the escape never happened. The prisoners who had been thought to plan the escape were

disciplined and harassed with more pushups and toilet cleaning.

At some point, even the prisoners who were thought of as role models, those who obeyed all of the guards' commands were being punished. Going to the bathroom was considered a privilege rather than a necessity, and those who acted out against the guards were made to urinate and defecate in a bucket in their cell.

By the end of the experiment, there was no unification among prisoners or guards. The guards had won complete control over all of their prisoners and were using their authority to its greatest extent. One prisoner had even gone as far as to go on a hunger strike. When he refused to eat, the guards put him into solitary confinement for three hours (even though their own rules stated the limit that a prisoner could be in solitary confinement was only one hour).

Prisoners and guards had rapidly adapted to their roles, stepping beyond the boundaries of what had been predicted and leading to dangerous and psychologically damaging situations. The planned two-week study into the psychology of prison life ended after only six days due to emotional trauma being experienced by the participants. The students quickly began acting out their roles, with "guards" becoming sadistic and "prisoners" showing extreme passivity and depression.

In his 2007 book *The Lucifer Effect*, Zimbardo says that humans cannot be defined as good or evil because we have the ability to act as both depending on the situation. "Good people can be induced, seduced, and initiated into behaving in evil ways. They can also be led to act in irrational, stupid, self-destructive, antisocial, and mindless ways when they are immersed in 'total situations' that impact human nature in ways that challenge our sense of the stability and consistency of individual personality, of character, and of morality." He also notes that we as humans wish to believe in unchanging goodness of people and our power to resist situational and external pressures and temptations. Zimbardo discusses that peer pressure, the desire to be 'cool,' the fear of rejection, and simply being a part of a group are the focal points to acting contrary to your character.

Ethical concerns surrounding the famous study often draw comparisons to the Milgram experiment, which was conducted in 1965 at Yale University by Stanley Milgram, Zimbardo's former high school friend. Stanley Milgram conducted research on obedient behavior in 1965 that embraced situational forces.

Milgram had "teachers" that delivered mock electric shocks to the "learner" for every wrong answer that was given in a multiple-choice test. The teachers, however, did not know that the electric shocks were not real, and still delivered them to the learners. At the end of the experiment, 65% of men aged 20–50 complied fully up to the very last voltage. In the same room as the teacher, there was a "confederate" that kept tabs on the teacher and if they were delivering the shocks to each wrong answer. In the beginning of the study, participants signed a waiver that clearly explained the ability to opt out of the experiment and not deliver the shocks. But with the surprising result rate of teachers who did continue to shock the learners, there was a situational force. The situational force that influenced the teachers to continue was the voice of the confederate egging them on by phrases such as, "I advise you to continue with this experiment" or "I am telling you to continue delivering the shocks" and the one that caught most teachers was "You must continue with the shocks." Although the teachers knew that they could leave the experiment at any point in time, they still continued

when they felt uncomfortable because of the confederate's voice demanding they proceed.

Both Milgram's and Zimbardo's experiment tested situational forces on an individual. Both results concluded that irrational behavior compared to one's character is plausible for any human because we have both tendencies in our nature. Both studies are frequently cited as examples of psychological experiments that were conducted in the mid-20th century that have serious ethical problems involving the treatment of human experimental participants. Both studies probably could not receive approval today from any university board of ethics.

According to Zimbardo there are 7 social processes that grease "the slippery slope of evil":
• Mindlessly taking the first small step
• Dehumanization of others
• De-individuation of self (anonymity)
• Diffusion of personal responsibility
• Blind obedience to authority
• Uncritical conformity to group norms
• Passive tolerance of evil through inaction or indifference

Source: Wikipedia

3 Generational shifts in the Netherlands

Successive generations in life stages

A generation consists of fifteen connecting years of birth, for instance the members of the Protest Generation were born between 1940 and 1955. Every fifteen years, a new generation comes into being, and at the same time the older ones enter their next life phase.

Generations succeed each other in life stages in a continuing process. For instance, the first cohort of the youngest generation, the Conscious Generation Z, entered their first life phase – childhood – in 2000. The last cohort of this generation entered this first life stage in 2015. This means that this youngest Dutch generation was fully represented within society by 2015 and succeeded the former generation in the phase of childhood, the Authentic Generation Y (1985-2000). In a parallel process in the other phases, new generations succeed the former ones. This is called a generation shift.

Why this shift takes place in a rhythm of fifteen years requires further research. Several important European thinkers who wrote about generations in the last two centuries mentioned this rhythm (see fig. 3). The Dutch classification of generations and its characteristics based on this rhythm of fifteen years is recognized by well over three-quarters of the Dutch population, as I mentioned in chapter 2.

What are life stages?

Life stages are fifteen-year periods in a life cycle that are marked by specific personal and professional development. Every life stage is largely determined by the consequences of age, such as biological effects, and effects of life experience. People who are in the same life stage will have about the same sort of vital questions. The effects of life stages are visible in:

1 The biological development of a person, measured from childhood to old age.

2 The way people shape their life stage, for instance as a new generation of seniors.

3 Vital questions: in childhood other questions are more important than in old age.

4 The development of (work) life experience and expertise. In fig. 9, you will find more details about the effects of life phases.

Individuals go through all the above stages, and each person handles this in a particular way, a way that they consider useful. Most individuals share life questions with their contemporaries during these stages. Through interaction among peers, individuals within a generation influence each other's lives. Interaction within a generation is most intense during the first stage of life and during the first years of the second life stage.

Building on the foundation that is created in the interaction with their parents and by the way they are brought up, interaction with peers is a next step in the development of characterizing (re)actions with respect to the vitality of the surrounding culture. You could see it as new social trends that are seeded in childhood and become steadier along the way. For instance, with every new generation in the Netherlands, females have more influence on males. This is affecting the way children are raised. Each existing generation is more feminine than the previous one. Macho behavior is becoming outdated. Feminine behavior is fading in and macho behavior is fading out. This is creating more feminine organizations and a more feminine society in the Netherlands.

With every life stage that passes, a person's work and life experience and the power to influence the surrounding culture increases. During the leadership stage between 45 and 60, the ability to influence the surrounding culture is strongest.

Life stage	Vital questions	Important events/ Social role	Biological effects < = Decrease > = Increase
Old age 75-90	How can I stay healthy and enjoy my life?	Increasing dependency on other people to help with everything they cannot do by themselves anymore. (Great-)grandparent	< locomotion < verbal skills < ability to solve problems and to make decisions > wisdom
Senior 60-75	What have I built so far and what do I still want to do in life?	Great amount of life and/or work experience. Better overview The ability to pass on the wisdom they acquired from experience to others. Responsibility for the following generations. Grandparent.	> life experience/better overview < mental flexibility < the ability to reason inductively > knowledge of the world and social insight > vocabulary > emotional stability
Leadership 45-60	In what way will I influence my environment and handle my responsibilities?	Biggest influence on environment. People in this life stage surpass self-interest. They have developed routines and they commit to the decision they have made. Their children have left home.	> social insight < eyesight < muscular strength < sense of hearing > influence on (working) environment > life and/or work experience
Medior 30-45	In which direction is my life going and does this feel steady to me?	Increasing influence on environment. Need for independence. Increasing independence. Raising children.	< quickness of reaction and speed of thinking < physical condition < perceptual rapidity > the ability to solve social problems > the ability to reason inductively > life and/or work experience > influence on (work) environment
Junior 15-30	What do I want to do in my (working) life? With whom do I want to maintain relations?	Making personal as well as professional connections. Birth of children. Sort of dependent. Learning.	Physical development has been completed > emotional development > mental development
Childhood 00-15	Where can I play and with whom?	Growth and development. Playing and learning. Dependency on environment.	> physical development > emotional development > mental development

Fig. 9 Stages of working life and their age-related effects

Some evolutionary changes take one, some take two or three life phases to materialize. For instance, the process of democratizing organizations by the Protest Generation in the Netherlands took three life stages. It started in the 1960s and reached its peak around 1994. Some fundamental changes need more generations to implement them in a process of long-term renewal of a cultural pattern. For instance, the way we deal with diversity and conflicts is changing. This seems to lead towards a multicultural Dutch society and a more peaceful world. This is not just a bold claim by an idealistic scientist. These evolutionary developments are backed up by data. They are the result of interactive processes in and between generations. It is not a straight-line development, but a process with ups and downs.

A generational shift

We can speak of a fulfilled generational shift as soon as all generations have made it to the next life stage, and have left the former stage. These generations simultaneously start to shape their life in the next phase in their own characteristic way, which is different from the previous one. For instance, the Dutch Protest Generation was idealistic and stimulated democracy, while the next one, the Dutch Connecting Generation X, is realistic and stimulates 'multicracy'. These differences in attitude impact on the way they behave in the leadership phase, or in other words how they fulfill this phase. Every generation shapes new ways of elderhood, seniorhood, leadership, mediorhood, juniorhood and childhood.

The most recent generational shift in the Netherlands, but probably also in Europe and other so-called Western economies, took place between 2000 and 2015. A shift starts with the first cohort of every generation that moves on to the next life stage and ends after 15 years with the last cohort entering that same life stage. The current generational shift started in 2016 end will last until 2030.

In what way a generational shift affects the existing culture can become visible about halfway into a shift in communities in which people and generations assume an open attitude towards each other. The effects of the current shift in the Netherlands started to become visible from approximately 2008. In communities where interaction between generations is less open and intensive, this process will be slower. Little and slow interaction between generations causes a time lag. This means that the effects of a generational shift will be noticeable later than halfway into the next shift. The effects of the generation shift that started in 2015 will be noticeable in the Netherlands approximately around 2023.

As I mentioned before, a generational shift produces two important effects. Well, I actually mean to say that these effects occur under the right conditions:

1 Every new generation in a particular life stage disposes of its own lifestyle and produces new social patterns. In other words: the members of a new generation live evolutionarily 'smarter' than the previous generation. This is the revitalizing effect of each different generation in fulfilling their life stage. For more information, I would like to refer to the next chapters about working generations in the Netherlands.

2 The generational composition changes as a whole. The influence of the oldest working generation – in 2016 the Protest Generation – decreases, whereas the influence of the youngest working generation – in 2016 the Authentic Generation Y – increases. The shift will also 'produce' a new generation of leaders that will lead the (working) world in a different way.

These effects fundamentally change the interaction and dynamics between generations and the spirit of the age in society. As I mentioned before, these culture-updating effects are (strongly) inhibited within many Dutch companies, despite the open culture in the Netherlands. The

Generations Years of birth	Actual life stage ages	Main focus of their energy and updates in the ongoing (organizational) culture
Pre-war Generation 1910-1925	Late old age stage > 100	Outside my research scope
Silent Generation 1925-1940	Old age stage 85-100	Outside my research scope
Protest Generation 1940-1955	Senior stage 60-85	Staying more active (thanks to their vitality); changing image of seniors. Keeping impact on society. Finding new ways to contribute to society, to explore their experience.
Connecting Generation X 1955-1970	Leadership stage 45-60	Connecting diversity and dialogue.
Pragmatic Generation 1970-1985	Medior stage 30-45	Speeding up learning and decision-making processes; interaction.
Authentic Generation Y 1985-2000	Junior stage 15-30	Freedom to shape their (working) life in an authentic way; equivalence.
Conscious Generation Z 2000-2015	Childhood stage 00-15	Consciousness of surrounding world (very open and hyper-realistic)

Fig. 10 Generations in the Netherlands: the last cohorts reached their current life stage in 2015 and the first cohorts entered their next stage in 2016.

demographic factor of working population aging seems to create this effect.

Generations in the Netherlands

Building on Henk Becker's classifications of generations, I made the classification in fig. 10, adding the youngest generations, the actual life stage and the main focus of their updates.

The main focus of their updates is the main characteristic of a generation. This main characteristic is linked to other new social patterns. For instance, speeding up decision-making processes is accompanied by interactive communication and debating (replacing the patterns of discussing). Speeding up learning processes is accompanied by sharing knowledge across company borders, in open systems (instead of keeping knowledge in closed systems and using knowledge as a hierarchical power), sharing knowledge through (social media) networks, focusing on developing your strengths (instead of weaknesses).

In the next chapters, I will describe the renewal brought by, and characteristics of, each Dutch working generation and of the next generation of juniors.

4 The Dutch Protest Generation as a new generation of vital seniors

Perhaps you have already noticed this in your personal environment: seniors of today are different from seniors of former generations. Many of them are more vital. The non-profit organization *PUM Dutch senior experts* is an active platform for senior experts who would love to participate in projects abroad. Frequently, Dutch seniors go into retirement via the front door of a company only to re-enter via the backdoor to work as a freelancer for that very same company. Or they offer their services via companies such as *Brown Cow* in Amsterdam in order to be able to give assistance to young entrepreneurs.

According to a study carried out by the Netherlands Institute for Social Research, an increasing number of seniors experience age discrimination. The Dutch Protest Generation seems to rise in rebellion again. Most members of this generation feel like they are ten to twenty years younger than they actually are and they want to be treated that way. An increasing number of vital seniors from the Protest Generation are focused on:

- Continuing to participate actively in the (working) community and contribute in a useful way
- Working within flexible hours, without any pressure of time
- Regaining their own passion: they want to do something they are passionate about and they want to do things they are good at
- Making better use of their acquired experience and gaining the recognition they deserve
- Finding ways to pass on their expertise to younger generations, particularly Y
- Finding ways to work in harmony with the younger generations, particularly Y. This gives them satisfaction and keeps them young

Point of particular interest: in order to work in harmony with the younger generations, seniors from the Protest Generation need to let go of many outdated patterns, such as 'explaining something on and on, having vague discussions, the belief that a senior always knows best, trying to get everyone to agree on something (the Dutch have a verb for this, 'polderen', which means talk with each other till you agree) striving to obtain a majority in order to reach a decision'. This means that the seniors who want to stay active in work need to transform (refresh) their outdated and deep-rooted routines.

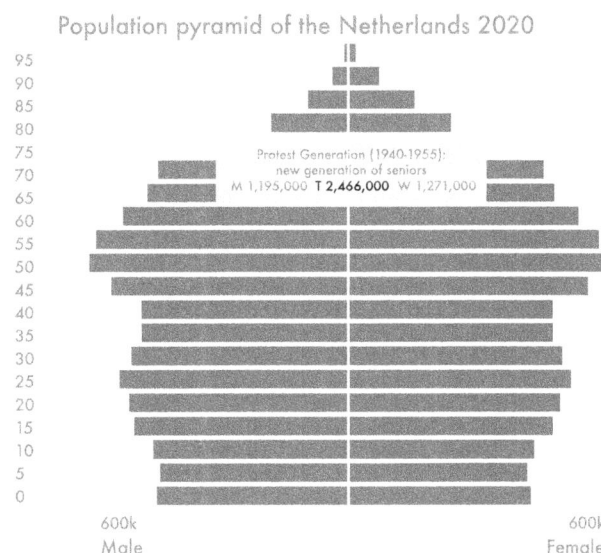

Fig. 11 The Dutch population pyramid of 2020 and the Protest Generation

The population pyramids of the last decades in the Netherlands show that not – contrary to popular belief – the Protest Generation, but the Connecting Generation (1955-1970) is the largest generation. It is, however, a very passionate and rather straightforward generation. In the 1960s, the members of the Protest Generation used their boldness to protest boisterously against the very authoritarian leaders of that time. These noisemakers actually belonged to a relatively small group that was concentrated in Amsterdam, spread

The Dutch polder model is characterized by the tripartite cooperation between employers' organizations, unions and the government. These talks are embodied in the Social and Economic Council of the Netherlands (Dutch: *Sociaal-Economische Raad*, SER). The SER serves as the central forum to discuss labor issues and has a long tradition of consensus, often defusing labor conflicts and avoiding strikes.

The current Dutch polder model is said to have begun with the Wassenaar Accords of 1982, when unions, employers and government decided on a comprehensive plan to revitalize the economy by reducing working hours and pay on the one hand, and creating more jobs on the other. This polder model, combined with a neoliberal economic policy of privatization and budget cuts has been held to be responsible for the Dutch economic miracle of the late 1990s.

Fig. 12 The polder model

over several universities. This is something we observe more often. Energetic, articulate students who demonstrate in capital cities as a front group against leaders or systems that represent outdated routines within a certain culture. This often goes hand in hand with much unrest.

Forming the new generation of working juniors in the 1960s, the Protest Generation primed the democratization of organizations. From the year 1963 onwards, juniors from this generation started to join unions and seniors from older generations started to support the Protest members more and more. This led to shrinkage of the gap between employees and leaders and to the famous polder model. Around the year 1994, this very successful model was noticed abroad. At the time, former union leader Wim Kok was prime minister of the Netherlands. The world wanted to know how we had managed to establish stability and economic prosperity in our society.

Until their leadership life stage, the Protest Generation had not only been strongly focused on democratizing our society and creating consultative structures and decision-making policies, they had also restructured our working community, kept on creating big organizations that kept on growing and created departments and suitable settlements for each and every problem. The growing number of meetings was focused on obtaining a majority for their proposals. The minority was persuaded to go along with the crowd, with the mainstream. Many leaders were generally very convinced that they were in the right and established committees with suitable experts to support their 'brilliant' ideas. Using smart communication strategies, leaders from the Protest Generation seduced people to agree. Managers of big organizations enjoyed high social status.

The expiration date of many of these patterns was around 1 January 2000. As early as in the late 1990s, younger generations started to consider the polder model and its 'meeting methods' as slow and vague. Much-heard criticism at the time was that the polder model does not produce enough concrete results, takes ages, involves a lot of nonsense and just isn't going anywhere. Around the year 2000, the polder model and its accompanying habits were losing their appeal. This coincided with the start of a generational shift. The younger generations found the leaders of the Protest Generation to be too idealistic, too eager to send out a message and too keen on status. Unions were increasingly seen as sluggish, introverted and narrow-minded organizations. Young generations started to avoid these outdated institutions.

When I look back from a generational perspective, I observe that the attitude of a large number of Protest members was not open-minded enough towards the feedback and impulses of renewal of the younger generations. In-depth interviews with thirty of these leaders and several generational experiments, conducted between 1993 and 2000, showed that they did not see the differences between their own generation and the Pragmatic Generation, which entered in

Increasing criticism of leaders from the Protest
Generation by younger generations after the
year 2000

"Leaders from the Protest Generation are rather dominant people. They do not give us enough space and they do not trust us enough. They tend to seclude themselves and do not listen very carefully. They are rather self-involved and somewhat stubborn; they do not seem to notice us. They talk a lot but they do not come into action. They are often busy making vague idealistic plans instead of giving concrete directions about what needs to be done. They can talk for hours about abstract matters. Their narrow-mindedness is quite irritating. They often behave in an authoritarian manner, as people who really think that they know the truth; they often keep some distance." (Bontekoning, 2012).

In their book *Bye Bye Baby Boomers* (2010), Paul van Liempt and Paul van Gessel, both members of Connecting Generation X, write with a zip of frustration: "Leaders from the Protest Generation are boisterous, self-satisfied people, who love to speak in long monologues. They are of the opinion that they invented everything, that they created heaven on earth and that nothing original can possibly be established by the generations that follow. They are convinced of the fact that, it almost seems like an obsession, society is 'makeable'. They have sealed this society tightly in order to do so. Everything needs to be handled from a central point. A prohibitive welfare state needs to be established. All of this has led to one big, irrepressibly bureaucratic mess. They pretended that they had established a world full of democracy and participation, while in reality, they forced through their romantic, utopian ideals. They created a relentless culture of bank bonuses and they saddled naïve customers with opaque products that were filled with lies and hot air."

Fig. 13 Criticism of Dutch leaders from the Protest Generation

the 1990s as a new generation of juniors. They did have the feeling that there were differences, but they were unable to identify them, not even when they had children from this young working generation. The culture-renewing value was not being acknowledged at all and therefore it was not being supported. It was not that they were unwilling to do so, but they just did not see or understand what happened. The small number of seniors who noticed and worried about energy loss and adaptation from juniors to the current culture did not know what to do.

Too many leaders from the Protest Generation had been clinging to their leadership position for too long. In 2010, a leading Dutch newspaper, De Volkskrant, published a top 200 of the most influential people in the Netherlands. Of these 200 influential people, 72% were members of the Protest Generation and 90% of them were male. There were not enough leaders from the Protest Generation that actively supported their successors from Generation X in taking over leadership in time. The leaders from the Protest Generation were almost unable to point out the characteristics of the next generation of leaders. They lacked understanding of the evolutionary value of the upcoming new generation of leaders. This is one of the reasons why many outdated patterns are still present in many Dutch organizations. We can also look at this from a different point of view. The younger generations have kept quiet for too long. They just stood there and watched, perhaps intimidated. They complained about outdated patterns to each other, but in general they did not express their feelings directly to the leaders of the Protest Generation. 'They don't want to listen to any of our complaints,' is a much-heard complaint. Whenever I encouraged these young people to express their opinion during my generation action research, leaders from the Protest Generation were astonished. 'Why have you never said anything before?' was their reaction. 'Your generation is better educated than ever, you are articulate young people, you have excellent public speaking skills, and even now you have not said anything about all of this before. That is incomprehensible and also weak.' The younger generations too often failed to wake up the members of the Protest Generation and to open their eyes to the need for renewal. The closed and distant attitude of many male leaders from the Protest Generation discouraged many juniors to open their mouths. The interpretation of this attitude by juniors was that their bosses did not want to hear their criticism and feedback. Many leaders from the Protest Generation said: 'If they do not protest, I assume everything is going well. But the Pragmatic Generation was simply not as noisy as their parents. Interaction between the juniors and their leaders was minimized and not open. Basically, neither talked about what was really going on in their minds and hearts. The interpretations of each other's behavior lead to misunderstandings. This blocked or at least delayed the updating process by the new generation of juniors and caused an increasingly outdated culture. Did this silence and withholding of necessary renewal of outdated routines contribute to a system crisis at the beginning of the 21st century?

Many scientists in the current decade are talking about a system crisis, meaning that important systems are at the end of their life cycle and need to be renewed. This could be because the younger generations did not get or did not take the chance to renew the outdated social patterns in these systems, for instance in banks. Culture is sometimes considered as the 'weak side' of an organization, but when you bump your head on this kind of matter, you hit a very hard wall. It can also feel as if you are swimming against a strong tide, making you think that there is not a chance in the world of you getting anywhere.

Male members of the Protest Generation have developed the polder model and its accompanying habits. Women of this generation did not have any influence on this development. Many of these women started working after their children had left home. Video recordings of the interaction in small groups of the Protest Generation in diverse organizations, dating from around the year 2003, show that many

women of this generation placed themselves second to men. Video recordings made after 2007 show that this kind of behavior is going through a transformation. Women within the Protest Generation are gaining more influence on their male peers. Generally, women from the Protest Generation are noticeably more vital than their male peers. This seems to be an important cause for this development. Another cause can be that, analogously, an increasing number of men from the Protest Generation have started to let go of outdated patterns. They are becoming increasingly susceptible to the influence of others.

Differences between the Protest Generation and the preceding generation of seniors

The differences between the Protest Generation and the preceding generation of seniors – the Silent Generation (1925-1940) – form the necessary ingredients for renewal of the existing culture. The members of this new generation of seniors, the Protest Generation, give a unique twist to their seniority, a twist that characterizes their generation. This process is still going on and its contours are becoming visible. The outcome of all this depends on the mutual interaction among peers of this generation. Will it become a trend for seniors to carry on working after they reach retirement age? Will they experience this as a way to stay vital? The outcome also depends on the mutual interaction between older and younger generations. Will juniors experience the wisdom of the oldest working generation as beneficial? As the number of positive experiences increases, more seniors will carry on working after they have reached retirement age. It seems as if the real challenge for the members of the Protest Generation is to change the outdated image of seniors that exists within a lot of organizations. Within many organizations, the current image of seniors and HR policy for senior employees is generally based on the experience with the previous generation of seniors: 'When you are about sixty years old, you start making preparations to wrap up your active working life.' However, a growing percentage of members of this new generation of seniors wishes to reorient their career and are occupied by the question of how they can keep on actively contributing to working life and to society.

The number of seniors who wish to carry on working has doubled to 62% in 2012, according to the Netherlands Institute for Social Research. This goes especially for people whose jobs do not involve heavy physical labor. Seniors whose jobs do involve heavy labor do not intend to keep on working. These are mostly employees with a lower degree of education. However, highly educated people in physically, mentally or emotionally taxing jobs also do not wish to carry on beyond their retirement age. Even though many of these seniors often feel like they are fifteen years younger than they actually are, they experience the effects of their current life stage. Their level of work energy decreases, just like their physical abilities (fig 6). For most of these seniors, an important question is how to use their energy in a smart way. This comes to the fore in their desire to do something that they are passionate about, as this generates work energy. Seniors feel the urge to stop doing things that drain away their work energy. Seniors who indicate that they wish to carry on working, often mention that they do not want to work in the same way as they used to and not at the same organization. They want to be their own boss. They want to be able to manage their own agenda and to plan their own working hours. They are tired of the bureaucracy, the long meetings and the 'cold' managers who are only interested in the organization's output in terms of figures and statistics. It is interesting that the juniors from Generation Y also consider these same factors as things that generate and drain work energy respectively. Furthermore, seniors are wondering how they can make the most of their acquired expertise in the (near) future and

how they will be best able to pass this on to young people, especially on to members of the new generation of juniors: Generation Y.

Over the last five years, I have studied interactions between the seniors and juniors of this time at various organizations. I wanted to find out whether the youngest and the oldest working generation would be able to work in harmony with each other. In the beginning, I presumed this could become a difficult thing to accomplish. The fact that struck me was that many seniors often turned out to consider Generation Y as the most charming generation with which to collaborate. 'They keep us young,' they said. 'They are so sincere and spontaneous, I love it!'

To my surprise, the youngest working Generation Y admitted to preferring to work with the experienced seniors from the Protest Generation, because 'we can learn so much from them!' During my experiments at several companies, I had small groups of juniors from Generation Y work together with small groups of seniors from the Protest Generation in order to explore the reason for such a remarkable connection. These experiments showed the following common ground between these two generations:

1 A shared appreciation of freedom and flexibility in the workplace, being able to work in your own way.

2 Not wanting to adjust to the existing culture. Protest Generation: 'When we started as juniors in the 1960s, we did not adapt to the existing culture. We notice the same attitude in your generation. The generations between us – X and the Pragmatic Generation – unwillingly adapted to the existing culture.'

3 Openly expressing one's opinions. Both generations said to the other generation: 'Your generation openly expresses the way you truly feel about things.'

4 Learning from each other. Y: 'We can learn so much from your enormous amount of acquired expertise.' Protest Generation: 'We like to pass on our wisdom to your ge-

neration and we need you to show us how to let go of our outdated routines and how to keep ourselves fresh.'

An interesting similarity between seniors with different levels of education was the feeling of pride they had in what they had built over the past decades: the economic successes and growth of their company, for example. And sometimes, the 'visible pain' they felt about the downfall their company had suffered from as a result of the crisis. Young people do not feel this connection to a company. They are more focused on their own development and on finding a challenge in their job. When young people feel proud of something, this is usually brought about by their own contribution to the company and from the way in which their company contributes to society.

So there is no generation gap between the oldest and the youngest working generation?

Yes, sometimes there is a gap. The more a senior from the oldest working generation adopts a grumpy and non-vital attitude, the bigger the gap between them and the Y juniors. This attitude reveals itself in remarks such as: "You just keep quiet until you have been at this company for a while; you'll see how we work here as you go,' with a somewhat cynical undertone. Or: 'Hey kid, save your spontaneity for playtime. At this company, we are used to working seriously.' The gap arises in a very literal way; young people start to go out of their way to avoid their grumpy old colleagues. The seniors, for their part, become even more grumpy and distant towards young people, saying things like, 'Young people nowadays, they don't know anything; they cannot accomplish anything. Yes, well, they can sit around, staring at their mobile phones. They do not listen anymore and they have become shameless.'

Between vital seniors and the current generation of juniors, a completely opposite development is taking place. They feel most connected when they feel 'passionate' about the same profession and experience an open attitude towards each other. In the Netherlands, we have a television program that shows this phenomenon very well. It is called '*Ali B op volle toeren*', which means '*Ali B at full speed*'. Ali B is a Dutch rapper and artist who, in this program, unites young Dutch rappers such as Kleine Viezerik, Winne and Negative with artists who were popular in the 1960s, such as the famous Dutch singers Rob de Nijs, Anneke Grönloh and Boudewijn de Groot. Ali B has these artists rewrite each other's songs and perform it in front of the original singer, creating some memorable moments and exceptional musical innovation. Old songs get 'pimped' and new songs become more profound and filled with wisdom. This is touching and moving.

The Protest Generation and spirit of the age during their childhood, 1955–1970

From 1950, the Dutch economy grew steadily (largely thanks to aid provided under the Marshall Plan), especially the agricultural industry and the construction industry. The spirit of modernism and progress during the first decades after the World War II strengthened the sense that the world is 'makeable'. Production machinery had been destroyed for a large part and infrastructure was in ruins. There was a lot to repair and to improve.

The large number of momentous 'firsts' strengthened the perception of a world full of possibilities for the young members of the Protest Generation. In 1952, the Netherlands saw its very first television broadcast, followed in 1959 by the building of the first subway line (Rotterdam), the first issue of the Dutch football magazine *Voetbal International*, the first TV commercial, the first nude scenes on television, the first jet plane for KLM (Royal Dutch Airlines), the introduction of the 5-day working week with Saturday as 'a day off', the introduction of the contraceptive pill, the first

1959
John F. Kennedy is elected as the 35th president of the United States.
1961
First human being travels in space.
Construction of the Berlin wall, cold war between 'East and West'.
1963
Martin Luther King delivers his famous "I Have a Dream" speech.
John F. Kennedy is killed.
The Beatles release their first album.
1964
The Rolling Stones release their first album.
Nelson Mandela imprisoned on Robben Island.
Release of the first James Bond movie.
1968
Martin Luther King is killed.
The Club of Rome is founded; increase of overall environmental awareness.

heart transplantation, the first kidney transplantation, and the first men on the moon.

The first television broadcast in the Netherlands, which aired in the year 1952, enlarged everyone's outlook on the world. Anglo-American consumption culture breezed into the Netherlands. Around 1955, rock and roll music broke through. A new generation of young people, the members of the Protest Generation, started rebelling against the existing lifestyle and moralities and authorities. The music and style of Elvis Presley, Bob Dylan, The Beatles and the Rolling Stones chimed perfectly with this rebellious attitude. This stimulated the emerging feeling of freedom. In 1956, women gained (full) legal capacity. Cities were growing steadily.

More and more members of the Protest Generation took the initiative to wrestle themselves out of the grasp of authoritarian leaders. They started by organizing demonstrations as students, but they increasingly developed democratization, emancipation, decolonization and secularization. Tradition-

al religious and social-political barriers in the Netherlands started to break down. Gradually, employers started allowing employees to influence the working environment. Managers started to organize meetings to evaluate progress within the organization, and employee participation became normal. Communications between 'bosses and workers' became more informal.

In 1963, a large natural gas field was discovered in the northeast of the Netherlands. This field yielded up to around six billion euros per year for the state of the Netherlands from 1970 until recently[1]. This enabled our government to bankroll the building of a welfare state. Could it be an explanation for the somewhat paternalistic attitude of many leaders from this generation?

The wedding of Princess Beatrix of the Netherlands to Claus von Amsberg in 1966 was briefly disturbed by a smoke bomb, thrown by demonstrators protesting against the marriage of the future Dutch queen to a German man. Claus eventually became a very popular prince.

In 1968, the Dutch 'Mammoth Act' opened the education system up to all strata of society.

In 1969, students had a sit-in at the Maagdenhuis, the administrative center of the University of Amsterdam, demanding more democracy at the university.

Members of the Protest Generation were – and they still tend to be – focused on what is going wrong at an organization. Mistakes need to be corrected and the culprit needs to be pointed out. Over many decades, employers and employees have used performance reviews to discuss weaknesses and how to overcome and to improve these weaknesses. Many seniors still struggle when it comes to identifying their strengths. They tend to react somewhat shyly and guardedly by saying typical things like, 'It is hard to say something like that about myself. It is up to others,

1 Recent earthquakes in the area of the gas field have forced the Dutch government to reduce gas production (2015).

who know me well, to answer that question.' The fact that members of the Protest Generation have trouble saying out loud what their strengths are does not mean that they do not have a clue about their strengths. It is 'just not up to me to name them,' seniors will often say. They are not used to thinking about their strengths. They are used to looking at their weaknesses and mistakes. For a long time, it has been a habit of members of this generation to disguise or to deny mistakes and to make things seem better than they really are. Fairly often, this turns out dramatically. A poignant example is the child sexual abuse within Catholic institutions in the 1960s that recently came to light. Today, we are used to revealing these kinds of things, but for a long time it was expected from us to keep such information to ourselves: 'You shouldn't air your dirty laundry in public.' Everyone just accepted this and went along with it.

A few years from now, when we look back upon the underlying causes of the global economic crisis, perhaps this persistent habit of hiding mistakes could turn out to be an important one. Society is becoming more and more transparent, but even nowadays whistle-blowers have a tough time exposing wrongs. They are considered to be traitors, instead of early warners of destructive patterns.

Today, this generation of seniors contributes to the fact that workforces and society as a whole are aging gradually, in all European countries. Thanks to their vitality, they will live and work longer. This presents various challenges:

- How can we make sure that we will be able to keep paying pensions for all retirees while we are still dealing with the fallout from the economic crisis and while gas production in the Province of Groningen continues to be reduced because of safety and environmental reasons?
- How do we make sure that welfare costs do not skyrocket and become unaffordable?

And it throws up questions that are (almost) never asked:

Busting a persistent myth and probably a typical Dutch discussion

It is a persistent myth that the members of the Protest Generation have profited the most from the welfare state. It is assumed that 42 percent of the 10 percent of the highest incomes is earned by baby boomers. In 2008, 35 percent of 620 billion euros' worth of state pension benefits was meant for seniors over 65 years old. This group contains only three Protest Generation birth cohorts, namely those born between 1940 and 1943. The socio-cultural report of 2010, drawn up by the Netherlands Institute for Social Research, states that the members of generations that came after the Protest Generation, who were born between 1960 and 1990 – mostly members of Generation X and the Pragmatic Generation – have profited the most from public spending. Between 1950 and 1980, public spending increased by 27 percent. This happened under the guidance of the Silent Generation and despite the fact that all generations profited from this, Generation Xers and the Pragmatic Generation benefited the most.

Between 1980 and 2007, public spending dropped by 10 percent. A large part of this decline took place under the guidance of the Protest Generation. This decline will steepen sharply over the years to come, the consequences of which will be felt by all generations. In comparative terms, the generations that came after the Protest Generation make more money and their income keeps on rising over the course of their career, thanks to ever higher educational standards and growing economic prosperity.
We do not know yet how the economic crisis has affected us, and neither do we know what the consequences of the crisis have been for the income of the youngest generations. It is most likely that, instead of the Protest Generation, the Silent Generation (1925-1940) is the richest generation of all. However, this depends on the value of their shares and houses. It is hard to determine whether this statement is correct or not. Since the value of real estate has been fluctuating over the last decades, it is hard to tell to what extent members of the Protest Generation have profited – more than other generations – from rising house prices.

Fig. 14 A typical Dutch discussion about profits

- How will we succeed in keeping the many aging organizations up to date?
- How can the rich experience of the fast-growing group of seniors be useful in the years to come, and how can we best utilize and reuse this expertise and pass it on to the younger generations?

Possible solutions have been found in raising the retirement age and can be found in encouraging people to delay their retirement. There are firms in the Netherlands that help seniors find work, firms such as '*Oudstanding*' ('oud' means 'old' in Dutch), as well as companies such as Brown Cow that match experienced seniors with young entrepreneurs. PUM is a Dutch non-profit organization that makes the expertise of an increasing number of experienced pensioners available to companies in emerging countries that cannot afford to hire expensive consultants.

How will seniors from the Protest Generation be able to keep their organizations up to date?

Seniors who are not doing so already should adopt a receptive attitude towards the renewing influence of young generations and keep on supporting them actively when it comes to revitalizing a culture.

Try to offer all of your life and work experience to the professionals from younger generations in order to support them in finding their own way. Try to use experiences from previous reorganizations – also the negative ones – to enable yourself to handle matters differently than before. Not by trusting everything blindly, but by approaching matters consciously and confidently. Being open-minded towards younger generations' different ways of collaborating, learning and communicating can be quite confusing. Sometimes it can feel unnatural because it forces you to step out of your comfort zone, and to leave your old routines behind.

However, repeating worn and outdated patterns has a direct negative effect on collaboration between the older and the younger generations. In the beginning, it may seem easier to notice the things that should *not* be done: repeating those outdated patterns, rather than noticing what you *can* actively do to improve the situation. What you could do will become clear along the way. Focus on young people's reactions. If something boosts their level of work energy and an increasing number of members of the younger generations retain a fresh view, collaboration with seniors will most likely develop in a positive way. These positive reactions can serve to help motivate seniors. Being open-minded towards the working methods and feedback of young people stimulates renewal of your own routines. It makes you want to keep on revitalizing yourself. These effects often result in an increased level of work energy and it makes your working environment more fun. This increases the possibility of young people wanting to cooperate with you and liking it. They are not sensitive to age. They are sensitive to vitality. If you are a senior and you feel like you are adapting to the behavior of the younger generation, it usually means that something is going wrong. When you experience a decline in your work energy, this is the signal that, evolutionarily speaking, you are on the wrong path. It may help to reflect on what is not working for you, and to start doing what raises your work energy. It may help to identify and to find a way to overcome the problem when you share openly with juniors what you are going through there and then, during your collaboration with them. Once you have shared with them how you feel, healthy interaction and collaboration can be re-established, one that creates mutual work energy. When members of older and younger generations work together in a relaxed way, relevant and often intuitive senior wisdom usually floats to the surface automatically. Working in a relaxed way stimulates the functioning of your own intuition, which causes insights to float to the surface, insights you had no idea even existed in your subconscious memory. Reacting in an open and intuitive way – not with a "yes, but..." attitude – creates the possibility for young people to learn from it. Wisdom is something they recognize instinctively. Various experiments have shown that when a senior is close to revealing his or her wisdom, the alertness of young people visibly increases. The contrary is also true. When there seems to be no possibility of wisdom floating to the surface, seniors tend to lose the attention of young people. This happens, for example, when you start telling them what you accomplished during your working life. At best, members of your own generation consider your status as high, but this is hardly ever interesting to young people. They start to show attention as soon as you start sharing with them everything you discovered and learned during your working life. Especially if this is relevant for the situation this particular junior is in or when he or she is looking for solutions.

Sometimes it might be hard for you to collaborate with young people. For instance, when you start to doubt something and you are convinced of the fact that this is not the right way to go because your experience tells you otherwise. Not saying anything and giving the members of the younger generation the benefit of the doubt will turn out all wrong. It is a better idea to share your doubts, without imposing them, and to have an open mind on whether they are wrong or right. Especially when you articulate your doubts clearly and start searching for solutions together on an equal footing.

Letting go of outdated patterns

In order to achieve harmonious collaboration between seniors and members of younger generations, seniors need to let go of outdated patterns, such as having vague discussions, communicating in an abstract way, organizing long meetings with discussions and believing that you are the only person in the world who knows what is right and what is wrong. Making mountains out of molehills, demonstrating fanatically, focusing on what goes wrong in an organization instead of what is going well and pointing out a culprit for mistakes. Seniors also tend to attach great importance to someone's status and display formal and very serious behavior when it comes to work. Letting go of these routines can be very difficult and demands a large amount of self-contemplation! You can start by assuming a receptive attitude towards the new patterns of the young generation and to state this explicitly. For example, when you are convinced of the fact that young people can learn a lot from older people, and deny the fact that older people can also learn from young people, you are stuck in an outdated pattern. This attitude can keep young people from learning from your experience. If you are open to the idea that both generations can learn from each other, this fresh new attitude will stimulate juniors to open up to your experience. Members of the new generation of juniors of today – Generation Y – will not be open to learning from the experiences of seniors as long as seniors are not open to learning from members of Generation Y as well. The fresh new pattern is to learn from each other in a mutual and interactive way. It is of mutual importance that seniors are open to fresh new patterns of younger generations and that they are willing to integrate these patterns into their working lives. This is just as beneficial to seniors as it is to younger generations, as it is to their company. It ensures that seniors stay vital and it increases the possibility that members of the younger generation start to appreciate the seniors for their rich work and life experience. For the company, it diminishes the possibility that seniors 'walk away' at the end of their career with valuable experience.

Leaving behind the patterns that are 'deeply embedded in our brain', as Victor Lamme states, can be accompanied by strong feelings. These transformational processes can contain the following phases:

1) Denial: 'It is not as bad as it seems. It is just that they do not understand me.'

2) Reality. Letting reality get through to you – speaking about it with your partner who says: 'I actually understand those young people. Sometimes it just drives me crazy that you always want to be right.'

3) Confusion. Allowing yourself to be confused and starting to develop and adopt new patterns.

4) Integration. Integrating these new patterns into your existing routines. The visible appreciation in your environment strengthens this development. It seems like the members of the Protest Generation are the first members of a generation to have to deal with the 'necessity' of a transformation in their working life. They can accomplish this transformation by letting go of outdated patterns that are deeply embedded in their brain and replacing them with new ones. The motivation for this development can be found in seniors' willingness to accomplish energetic collaboration with younger generations.

Breaking through the image that seniors do not want to be active and that they do not want to learn new things.

Many members of the current new generation of seniors are caught in the outdated image of seniors in the minds of many (HR) managers and colleagues. This image is based on the previous generation of seniors, namely 'seniors do not want to stay active, let alone they do not want to start a new project or take up a new study. They want to cut down on their working hours; you need to spare them a bit.' This does not match the wishes of a growing part of this vital generation. Members of the Protest Generation want to stay active as long as they can, or at least be able to make their decisions on the matter. If a senior complains about the lack of appreciation he receives for his acquired experience, it reinforces the outdated image, such a reaction is an old pattern. A better approach is to state, loud and clear, that you want to

stay in the game, that you are open to new challenges, but that you want to build on your rich experience and do things you are passionate about, because, as these seniors state, 'I need to be selective in my activities since I do not have as much energy as when I was twenty years old, but I definitely do not feel like I am a sixty-three-year-old; I feel about 20 years younger.' You will receive more appreciation from the younger generations when you assume an open-minded attitude and when you are aware of your own responsibilities and qualities. These are fresh new patterns of today.

Reorienting towards 'passion'

Many seniors need to moderate their activity levels, because their energy levels decline as they grow older. Doing something you are passionate about and building on acquired expertise generates energy. Sometimes a senior needs a coach to rediscover his or her wisdom and to refind what makes life meaningful and what makes him or her energetic.

De-embitterment

It is difficult to stop someone from becoming embittered because it is hard to say, 'You are a bitter person, and I will help you get rid of your bitterness.' After all, no one turns bitter voluntarily. Your environment has not interfered either. Sometimes, this is because colleagues think it is the responsibility of a manager to interfere. It is something that just 'happened' to the embittered senior in question. He will not be able to break out of this negative spiral on his own; he needs support. Embittered seniors are often victims of the umpteenth reorganization of a company, in which they were moved into a role they did not want to be moved into. Outdated patterns that are repeated by people seem to be one of the most important sources of their embitterment. Repetition of outdated patterns causes a gap between the older and the younger generation; it causes health problems and a decline in the well-being of all people involved. Young people often give these seniors a wide berth. This only adds to the problem. The sooner they tackle an issue like this, the more likely it will be that seniors wake up and become aware of their outdated behavior and start to solve this problem.

This is also in seniors' interest. Not only do they stand in their colleagues' way, they especially stand in their *own* way. It is of economic importance as well; embittered seniors will most likely retire early and rack up extensive medical costs.

Demand for seniors might increase
There are at least three reasons to assume that demand for seniors will increase in the near future:
1 Our economy is expected to improve slowly. There is a good chance that this will create a labor shortage within a few years. The only age group within the working population that looks likely to grow, is that of the seniors.
2 Shouldering the different costs of population aging. It would be beneficial for seniors to carry on working, preferably even beyond the age of sixty-five.
3 The youngest working generation, Generation Y, claims to like working together with the vital seniors of the Protest Generation. Members of Generation Y feel connected to these seniors and they think they can learn a lot from them. Companies that expect to need Y juniors would be wise to keep employing at least a considerable number of vital seniors from the Protest Generation; especially seniors who are passionate about their profession.

5 The Connecting Generation X in the phase of leadership

It has taken them a while, but, in the Netherlands, Generation Xers are finally starting to occupy leadership roles at companies, in politics and at other institutions, replacing members from the Protest Generation. The announcement of the MT500 2014 management event organized by Dutch magazine *Management Team* underlines clearly how the Connecting Generation X will be renewing the concept of leadership, using the headline 'Alone is the New Together.' The announcement states, 'At this moment, we are part of a sharing economy. Nobody can make it on their own. Managers and companies need each other in every possible way, collaborating in a working environment, across a chain, in a multidisciplinary team. There is sometimes even collaboration with competitors. And what about innovation? All these things depend on a successful collaboration.'

Contrary to popular belief, the Dutch population pyramid shows that Generation X has the most members. Not only is this generation larger than the Protest Generation, it is also more successful, measured by level of education, salary and position in the same life stage. Initially, this generation was called 'the Lost Generation'. However, twenty years later it turned out that they were not lost at all. It is the most modest working generation. Compared to members of the previous generation, Generation X is generally less driven and outspoken. Their strength lies in their modesty and approachability. This attitude gives space to other generations to contribute in companies and also in society.

The connecting quality of Generation X's leadership may turn out to strongly affect the outcome of the economic crisis in the Netherlands.

Compared to previous generations, the Connecting Generation X (1955-1970) as a new generation of leaders is more focused on:

- Achieving results and sharing successes together
- Exploiting diversity constructively
- Connecting different points of view and different qualities
- Working together without anyone assuming a superior attitude towards the other
- Listening to other people's opinion and assuming an approachable attitude
- Using a coaching management style
- Facing reality – both weaknesses and strengths – and identifying what is going well
- Finding a balance between content and processes, between internal and external, etc.

Points of particular interest: members of Generation X are not always very clear about what they actually want, and they tend to become rather invisible to other generations. The current crisis demands visible leaders. We need that Generation X-style leadership, a kind of leadership that is up to date, to create a socially, economically and ecologically healthy culture. The outdated patterns that Generation Xers have taken over from their predecessors rather subconsciously and involuntarily are draining away work energy from themselves and other generations. These patterns contribute to the aging of our culture. How can we stimulate this generation to express their true strengths at work and in their leadership?

The majority of the members of Generation X are currently in the stage of leadership. Step by step, this generation has acquired the most influence on our (working) culture. Members of Generation X have been taking over many top jobs from the Protest Generation at many companies, at governmental institutions and in politics. The most energetic and prominent leaders from Generation X are typical products of this new generation. In politics, there is the young Prime Minister of the Netherlands, Mark Rutte and the Dutch Finance Minister Jeroen Dijsselbloem. The leaders of most Dutch political parties are Xers. In business, there are the CEOs Frans van Houten (Philips) and Wiebe Draijer (Rabobank), the successful businesswoman

Annemarie van Daale, and the union leader Ton Heerts. The coaches in charge of the Netherlands' big three soccer teams (Ajax, PSV and Feyenoord), mathematician and physicist Robert Dijkgraaf, who is a professor at the University of Amsterdam, and Leon Levy, Professor at the Institute for Advanced Study in Princeton, New Jersey, are also from Generation X. Female leaders of Generation X are upcoming, but not so visible yet.

Population pyramid of the Netherlands 2020

Connecting Generation (1955-1970): new generation of leaders	
M 1,790,000	T 3,583,000	W 1,793,000

600k Male — 600k Female

It has not been easy for these leaders to obtain their positions. In the Netherlands, loyalty towards these leaders is rather fragile. We are still accustomed to the previous generation of leaders; a generation that seemed to have everything under control and that publicly expressed their views in a very convincing way. These leaders were very present in our lives, and they knew how to sell their opinion, even

2 See for more information about my generation research methodology in the appendix

when they knew that they were not speaking the whole truth.

Analysis of video recordings[2] of small groups of Generation X in diverse Dutch organizations shows that women from Generation X are more able to influence men than women of the Protest Generation were in the leadership stage. This results in the fact that members of Generation X have a greater sense of appreciation for connecting qualities, that they show less macho behavior and that they pay more attention to processes in general. A remarkable quality of members of Generation X is their ability to focus on working *together*. They are interested in various points of view. In addition, this generation of leaders seems to only show themselves when this is really needed.

The luxury of early retirement will not be available anymore to Generation X in the Netherlands, and many will even work past retirement age. This means that Generation X will be the main driver of population aging and aging in organizations in decades to come. In turn, this means that it is of the utmost importance that the members of this generation stay vital in their working lives.

Members of this generation were faced with an economic crisis during the junior stage of their lives, in the late 1970s and the 1980s. Now, during their phase of leadership, they are confronted with an even deeper and broader crisis again. They are our new leaders. This is a remarkable fact. Thanks to the qualities of the members of Generation X, such as their ability to focus on achieving results together, to make optimum use of diversity and their focus on realism, the leaders of this generation have the potential power to pilot the people of the Netherlands through the current crisis. This development is still in the making and will become more and more visible in years to come. In 2016, the economic crisis in the Netherlands officially came to an end. Their leadership behavior will gain in support and confidence over the years. Aside from the fact that the

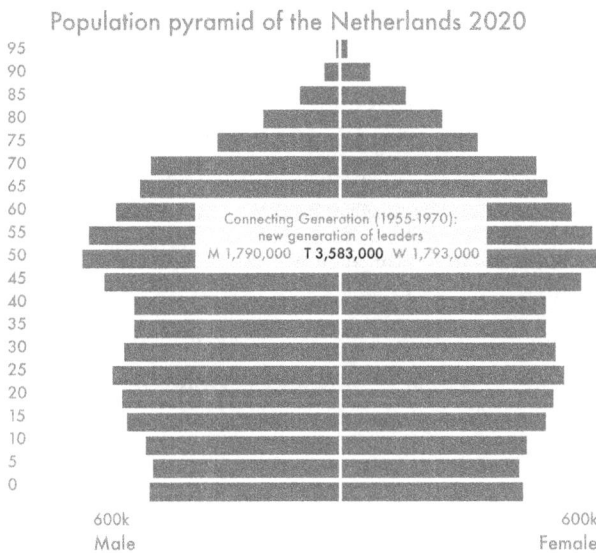

aforementioned potencies will continue to develop, the two biggest challenges for the members of this new generation seem to be:

1 To learn how to 'transfer' and strengthen contemporary ways of cooperating, communicating and leading at home, as parents of their Generation-Y children, towards the working environment.

2 To let go of (the remains of) outdated patterns that they have (subconsciously and involuntarily) taken over from the previous generation of leaders, such as hierarchy-based and bureaucratic behavior.

Last but not least: most Dutch Generation-X parents are very good educators of members of the Authentic Generation Y (1985-2000). According to the Multinational Time Use Study from Professor Gershuny of the University of Oxford (http://www.timeuse.org), Generation-X parents who have Generation-Y children, spend more than twice as much time raising their children than parents from the generation before them (Protest Generation as parents). My analyses of videos of groups of Generation-X parents, who were talking about the raising of their Generation-Y children, also showed many substantial qualitative differences with respect to the previous generation of parents. The relationship between Generation-X parents and their children is, among other things, more equal footed, closer and more open. Dutch Generation-X parents stimulate their children in a positive coaching way to be authentic and to find their own way. Their parenting style is reflected in the natural behavior of this new generation of juniors and their strong need for informal and 'face-to-face' contact. Research by UNICEF shows that Dutch Generation-X parents are doing a great job (see figure below). Their Generation-Y children are among the happiest of the world, not because they are spoiled, but because of the high quality and the quantity of the interaction between parents and children.

The Connecting Generation and spirit of the age during their childhood, 1970-1985

The spirit of the age during the years of youth of Generation X differs considerably from the spirit of the age of the Protest Generation. The economic boom of the 1960s made way for a recession around 1974, partly triggered by two international oil crises. This crisis lasted until 1984. Dutch politics focused on pay restraints, government budget cuts and the transformation of the private sector. Budget cuts at universities and limits on the number of students for several studies meant that many students from this generation could not start with a study of their first choice.
Perhaps, the recession reinforced the modest attitude of Generation X, but this attitude definitely emanated from the parenting style of the parents of Generation X: the law-abiding members of the Silent Generation (1925-1940). The typical realism of Generation X also contained a reaction to the idealism of the Protest Generation: X had found the world not to be as ideal as hoped.
In 1984, unemployment rose to 10.3% and youth unemployment to well over 17%. Many members of Generation X accepted a job below their educational level, decided to retrain or remained unemployed for a while. Newspapers published many articles about a 'Lost Generation'. The worried tone that was conveyed by the voice of Queen

Beatrix of the Netherlands during her Christmas address of 1985 was significant, as she uttered the following words: 'Solving the problem of youth unemployment is a challenge. All originality, all imagination and an all-out effort are needed to prevent a whole generation from becoming lost.'

The main themes in politics were decentralization of power, knowledge and income during the government of Prime Minister Joop den Uyl (1973-1977), and a no-nonsense mentality, government budget cuts and transformation of the private sector during the reign of Prime Minister Ruud Lubbers (1982-1994).

International events with (some) impact

1972   The report 'Limits for Growth' from the Club of Rome, an international think tank that deals with world issues, is published: this report was drawn up in order to alert people all over the world to the exhaustibility of fossil fuels and pollution

1973   The oil crisis began in October 1973 when the members of the Organization of Arab Petroleum Exporting Countries (OAPEC) proclaimed an oil embargo. The embargo came in response to countries such as the U.S., Canada, the UK, and the Netherlands supporting Israel during the Yom Kippur War.

1979   A second energy crisis gripped the world from the start of 1979. Iran's January revolution had seriously disrupted oil production in one of the most important exporters of the commodity. Oil prices rose from 12 to 33 dollars a barrel and the world was feeling the effects of an "oil shock".

1977   Apple introduced the first personal computer with monitor and keyboard

1985   Introduction of car telephone

In 1977, Henk Becker, who was Professor of Sociology at Utrecht University at the time, published a book called 'The Future of the Lost Generation'[3] in which he already anticipated the arrears in personal development and wage movements that he expected for Generation X. These arrears could not be repaired, as Becker stated. However, a study carried out at Tilburg University in the Netherlands in 1999 showed that this generation turned out to be not quite as lost as expected. In 2010, research carried out by the Netherlands Institute for Social Research also showed that earlier fears about the existence of an entire lost generation were unfounded. Members of Connecting Generation X feel like they have to work harder for success than members of the Protest Generation and the Pragmatic Generation did. Perhaps members of Generation X learned how to persevere, even if things did not necessarily go their way. They seem to have learned how to be conscious of the few possibilities they had at their disposal as well as how to make the most of these possibilities. They learned to be realistic and patient. This comes in useful now. They form our new generation of leaders, a generation that needs to guide us through the deepest crisis since 1929. Today, in 2017, we know that they have done exactly that, as we complete the economic recovery. However, new crises have already popped up: Brexit and cooperation in the EU, finding European answers to the stream of refugees, the climate crisis.

In the 1970s, the Netherlands started to become an increasingly multicultural country. The independence of Suriname after centuries of Dutch rule led to massive migration of people from this South American country to the Netherlands. Workers from Morocco and Turkey who had been brought to the Netherlands under a guest worker program or who had come on their own in the 1960s ended up staying. In the 1970s, these workers were joined by their wives

3 Original Dutch title: *De toekomst van de Verloren Generatie*

and children as part of a family reunification program. In this context, members of Generation X became aware of the importance of diversity and constructive ways to make use of differences. Growing diversity in Dutch society also brought polarization between right-wing and left-wing political parties around 1980.

The computer era had only just begun. In 1977, Apple launched the first successful personal computer with a monitor and a keyboard. In the early 1980s, affordable computers hit the market, which makes Generation X the last generation to grow up without computers.

How will Generation X be able to keep their organizations up to date?

Letting go of outdated patterns to which Generation Xers adapted automatically

Conversations with groups of Generation Xers at various organizations taught me that many members adapted their habits to the outdated elements in the existing culture as soon as they started working. The first cohorts entered the workforce around the year 1978.

In my generation experiments at numerous companies that had asked me how they could become more attractive to youngsters from Generation Y, I found that their parents, often the biggest generation at the company, know their children very well. However, they almost never used their experience with their children as a source for finding answers to their question.

I noticed that Generation X was generally overrepresented in my meetings at these companies. The first time this happened, I thought that they might not know their children very well or that they might have overlooked the fact that they know their children and their peers, Generation Y, even better than I do. To find out what was going on at the companies in question, I asked a small group of Generation

Xers who had children from Generation Y to come forward and talk with each other about typical features of their children's behavior. The audience could see what happened and hear what they said. After a couple of minutes we noticed that knowledge of Generation Y was indeed available at the company among the group of parents. So, I asked them to use their experience with Generation Y at home to answer the question of how to be an attractive company to those juniors. Although I had been brought in to answer that question, I felt they themselves were much better placed to answer it. I think the knowledge of parents based on their daily experience with Generation Y is deep knowledge. I rephrased the question for them: use your knowledge of your children to find the best way to support juniors at your company, who are, after all, peers of your children, in their personal and professional development. It only took them a couple of minutes to find the answers they needed. They seemed to have overlooked the fact that they know their children better than I do. Still, acquiring more knowledge of Generation Y might not instantly lead to the company becoming more attractive to Generation Y! This led me to the following question: 'You know what to do, but are you really doing what you identified as the best way to support Generation Y?' This question almost always created some uneasiness and produced different answers, ranging from 'Some level of hierarchical and formal behavior is just expected from you at an organization' to 'Without some hierarchy and strict rules and protocols it will become a mess' and 'I actually never realized I was acting that way.' We talked about this for a couple of minutes and ended up with some unexpected conclusions: 'At home, you, as parents from Generation X, have a very good relationship with and are highly appreciated by your children. You have the right attitude at home, but on the commute to work, your attitude changes into something that is not attractive to members of Generation Y. So you basically create the unattractiveness yourself. You disconnect from Generation Y somewhere on your way from home to work.' Some Generation-X parents said that they had a home button and an at-work button. The home button means: on equal footing, giving positive feedback, coaching their children in finding their own way, open communication, sharing emotions, informal and personal relationship. But as soon as they hit the at-work button, they enter a mode of hierarchy, formality, punishing mistakes, closed and formal relationships, not sharing emotions, ratio driven. At work, many leaders from Generation X repeat outdated patterns from former generations. They behave in a way that they would never behave at home. And if they were to unwittingly behave that way at home, they would instantly get corrective feedback from their children. Children are hypersensitive to outdated patterns and instinctively resist them.

We also did generation research with groups of members of Generation Y. The outcomes will be detailed in the chapter about Generation Y. When we were analyzing Generation Xers, in real time and on video, with these Generation Y groups, they said: 'Our parents do not act the same way at work as they do at home. Their behavior at work is much more formal, hierarchical, bureaucratic and close-mouthed.' When I checked the conclusion that they repeated outdated patterns by asking members of Generation X whether this kind of hierarchical and formal behavior at work energizes them, they invariably answered 'no'. This is a sign that they are repeating outdated patterns. At many companies, this is leading to the question of 'What can we do to be more attractive to the new generation of juniors.'

This brings us back to the question of how the members of Generation X can stay away from these outdated patterns. Many Generation Xers think that this is possible. It is not easy to define how they should do it. Earlier on in this book, when I discussed the Protest Generation, I mentioned something about transformation processes. These processes are about letting go of patterns that were vital in the previous century. Members of Generation X need to start letting go of outdated patterns that they involuntarily (and often) subconsciously took over from the generation before them. The solution to this cultural and generational puzzle can be found in a surprising area, namely in Generation Xers who have Generation-Y children. They should learn how to transfer the contemporary ways of cooperation, communication and leading that they developed at home to their working environment. In other words: they should not feel they have to switch to at-work mode on their way to work, but instead they should consciously stay in home mode. Initially, this may take some getting used to. It could help them if they realized that all generations, including their own peers, suffer from the repetition of those involuntarily and subconsciously adopted outdated patterns and would welcome new patterns of leadership.

It could be useful to raise this issue in leadership programs, where they can learn how to transfer their home communication and cooperation style to the workplace, as a method to update their way of leadership.

According to research carried out by UNICEF, Dutch children from Generation Y are among the happiest in the world. Not because these children are spoiled, but because their parents, from Generation X, take their job as educators very seriously and have close and open relationships with their children. They are very good parents, also in the eyes of their children, and seem to understand their children very well.

During the past year, I visited a few companies where people worked together and managed the company in a way that closely resembled the kind of collaboration and leadership we see in the family life of Generation-X parents with Generation-Y children. These routines consist of a mix of openness, equality, approachability, a lot of mutual confidence and personal contact, and a focus on achieving and sharing results together. The leaders were visibly and distinctly present, without feeling superior to their employees. They took up a rather coaching and guiding position. This was highly appreciated by all generations.

Sometimes, I decide to use a different approach. I ask Xer parents to compare their children's world to the culture of their company. One of the effects of being in their current life stage is that they know this culture very well. They know their company's culture as well as they know their children's world. I ask these parents the following question: 'Could you name three characteristics of your organizational culture that differ most from the world of your children?' My interviewees were able to answer this question within a couple of minutes. The top-three answers are almost always: top-down management, bureaucracy/working by obligatory protocols and a close-mouthed/formal attitude. At this point, people realize what the problem is, but they often tend to think that it is up to someone else to solve it. From this perspective, many Generation Xers fail to take their responsibility when it comes to updating their leadership style. The need to break through top-down management patterns is growing strongly at many Dutch organizations.

Show yourself and take charge

Generation X is the most modest generation of all. Just to be clear: this is their strength. This strength is connected with Generation Xers' need to work together without anyone assuming a superior attitude towards another. Members of other generations often criticize the fact that Xers remain too invisible. Other generations need visible and clear directions in processes, in which they need to feel involved. This leads to the question of how Generation Xers can make sure that they are distinctly present while working together without anyone assuming a superior attitude towards the other. In order to achieve this goal, members of Generation X can again try to transfer the skills they developed in their own

X/Y family life to the working environment. Most Xers lead their family in a clear way, while staying on an equal footing with their children. It seems to be an outdated idea that you can only lead people when you keep a distance (hierarchy, formality). In fact, we are seeing a change in the opposite direction in the Netherlands: we want to know our leaders in a kind of personal way. While this evolutionary change has already taken place in most Dutch young families, organizations are still lagging behind.

If Generation X does not succeed in 'renewing outdated routines of organizational cultures together' in their leadership phase, particularly at aging organizations, the negative effects will arise in different fields. Firstly, it will cause economic problems, as we will have to deal with outdated products and services. It will also cause social problems, as our confidence and optimism will fade away, and the tension between younger and older generations will mount. Thirdly, there are potential ecological repercussions. After all: if we are not even able to properly manage our own human energy – outdated patterns drain away work energy from all generations – how will we be able to manage the world's energy supply?

Exploiting the benefits of a diverse workforce

Our working community is becoming increasingly diverse, diverse in terms of disciplines, ethnic backgrounds, age and level of education. Or in other words, we are currently in the middle of a broad process of emancipation. All different groups in Dutch society and at their institutions want to be of equal importance and want to participate on an equal footing. To be able to see, hear and accept all these different influences, what is needed is an attitude and processes that differ greatly from those that served us so well during the democratization of organizations during the second half of the previous century. In those decades, the majority dominated the minority. In his first-ever speech as king, Willem-Alexander of the Netherlands coined the term 'participation society'. Which reflected that we are trying to find our way to achieving such a society where everyone participates, where all minorities in society and at organizations are accepted and respected. This fundamental change comes through interactive processes, also within generations. This is why people with a dissenting opinion need to speak up as well. This cultural change, in which adversaries of ideas are also heard and in which every minority contributes to developments, will only continue if it brings about evolutionary advantages for our community. A 'particpation society' will only continue if we are able to connect that diversity and to exploit it, and when the benefits are experienced broadly in society. This seems like quite a challenge to me. Our leaders from Generation X seem to have accepted this challenge. From this perspective, the leadership style of Barack Obama was an interesting one and might serve as an example. Despite the fact that he could not connect Republicans and Democrats in the U.S. in a constructive way, he can still be considered a symbol of diversity. He seemed to be intrinsically motivated to develop a leadership style that respects and appreciates diversity. We should not forget the fact that Generation X seems best capable to make optimum use of the vital power of different generations in order to keep (aging) organizations up to date. My research has shown that Generation X is very good at pointing out characteristics of other generations (Bontekoning 2007, 2010).

6 The Pragmatic Generation: an inhibited, yet accelerating generation

The professionals of the Pragmatic Generation have a strong focus on accelerating and concretizing the process of gathering and sharing knowledge, decision making, and learning. My various generational experiments, conducted at real-life organizations, showed that the members of this generation were able to reduce the lead time of these processes by at least half, by employing their pragmatic approach with support from senior colleagues. Roughly 15 billion euros is spent every year on meetings in the Netherlands. The strength of the Pragmatic Generation has the potency to cut this to about 7.5 billion. Slow and vague meetings consume most of their energy at work. At the same time, excessive meetings are also in the top 3 of biggest workplace energy drains for older Dutch generations! It is strange that this practical, accelerating strength of the Pragmatic Generation has not been actively supported by older generations. At most Dutch organizations, pragmatic efforts foundered on the stubborn outdated features of the polder model. This model was created in the 1970s and 1980s by the Protest Generation together with unions and contributed to social economic successes in the last century. However, the expiration date of many patterns of the polder model was 01/01/2000.

Certain parts of the polder model are deep-rooted and subconsciously repeated by older colleagues, even in 2016, despite the fact that the expiration date was sixteen years ago. Thanks to their increasing amount of acquired experience, the Pragmatic Generation, now in their medior phase of working life, seems better able to renew these outdated patterns. The stagnation of their updating has been a millstone around the Pragmatists' neck for a long time now, at least since they entered the workforce in the 1990s. However, they currently report more positive changes than ever. They are starting to become aware of the fact that other generations have also gotten sick and tired of those slow and vague deliberations during those long, useless meetings.

Compared to the previous generations, this new generation in the medior phase is more focused on:
- Arranging productive, quick, concrete and interactive meetings and processes of decision making and shared learning
- Sharing knowledge via e-networks, across organizational boundaries
- Learning new skills from doing work that challenges them, picking up knowledge as they go
- Taking their responsibility and being an independent employee
- Communicating interactively

Points of particular interest: to what extent did the members of this generation adapt to outdated patterns during their junior stage? In what way will the early loss of work energy and fresh views affect their attitude in their next stages of working life? Are they able to let go of the outdated patterns that they unwillingly repeated? To what extent has this enforced the outdating process of the cultures that they are a part of? In what way will this generation attempt to recover their generation's evolutionary power?

The Pragmatic Generation is the new generation entering the medior stage, the stage between the junior stage and the leadership stage. The generational effect will be determined by how the members of the Pragmatic Generation fulfill their working life during this stage, compared to previous generations. Being in the medior stage means that you have acquired enough experience to influence the working environment a little more and that this power will peak in the next stage. This generation will enter the leadership stage between 2015 en 2030. Halfway into that stage, the effects on the evolution of leadership will become visible. The number of female leaders will rise. The Pragmatic Generation is the first generation that shows equality between men and women in collaboration processes. For the first time in a Dutch generation, the average level of education of its female members is higher than that of its male members. The Pragmatic Generation has fewer members and is, on average, better educated than its predecessor. With this sharp rise in the level of education came an increasing desire to take up roles with real responsibility in the working environment. When they started their working life, in the 1990s, this quite often conflicted with the rather paternalistic attitude of the leaders from the Protest Generation.

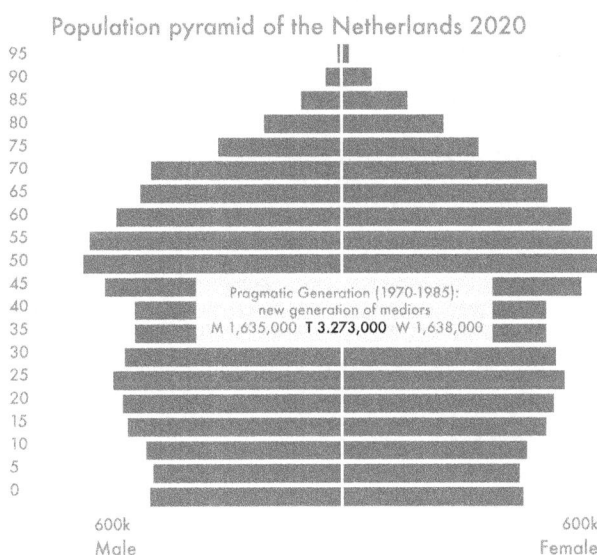

Population pyramid of the Netherlands 2020

Pragmatic Generation (1970-1985):
new generation of mediors
M 1,635,000 T 3.273,000 W 1,638,000

600k
Male

600k
Female

Fig. 18 The Dutch population pyramid and the Pragmatic Generation in 2020

The Dutch Protest Generation, i.e. the parents of the members of the Pragmatic Generation, encouraged their children to be independent. They stimulated their children by saying things like: 'Do your best, make sure you get a good education, make sure you can stand on your own two feet.' These parents were not only proud of the good education of their children, it also raised their social status in their own generation. They felt proud of good academic records of their children and they loved to share this with the people around

them. However, when things did not go as well, they often kept this quiet. Parents from the Dutch Protest Generation tend to have – often unspoken – high expectations of their children. This may have led to the fact that members of the Pragmatic Generation often aim for perfection.
The first cohorts of the Pragmatic Generation entered the business community as juniors around the year 1993. 'The polder model' was at its peak at that time and had instilled its quintessential habits, such as having long meetings and heated discussions in which participants tried to convince each other of being in the right.
I have seen many fresh-faced juniors from the Pragmatic Generation go stale very soon after entering an organization. This happened, for example, at Dutch organizations such as Philips, DSM, PTT Telecom, the fire brigade and the police. In the years that followed, I noticed the same process take place at about 85% of other bigger organizations. It broke my heart to see those young highly educated and talented juniors lose their fresh energy so quickly. To me, it seemed unhealthy, both for them and for their companies. It was a strong wake-up call for me[4]. I promised a group of young managers at the Dutch fire brigade that I would use all my talents to improve these processes of organizational culture renewal. It was the reason I started implementing the findings from my generational research in practice. At that time, I had no clue where it would lead. Eventually, it led to my PhD generation research and thesis in 2007, to five books about generations and many articles and master classes, as well as to generation projects in recent years. It raised awareness of the issue at many Dutch organizations. In recent years, increasing numbers of companies have started to search for effective solutions. It is a slow process

4 When I was a manager at the police force in the 1980s I noticed the value of intuition. My master's thesis (organizational psychology at the University of Utrecht, 1985) was titled 'The contribution of intuition in the process of strategic decision making'.

that requires a lot of patience. There is still a lot to learn and do, also at other aging companies across Europe. Spontaneous renewal of the existing culture by this former youngest generation got stuck in outdated patterns too often and too long. Typical reactions from these Pragmatists were, and continue to be: 'It is useless to swim against the tide,' 'Our time will come,' 'Gosh, all those meetings, so slow and vague, they do not seem to end and they lead nowhere,' 'Let's say you have a good idea. Firstly, you need to put it down on paper in order for the managers to discuss it with other managers in a meeting and if you are very, very lucky, in about two months you hear whether they will act on your idea or not,' 'And don't even start about all those opinions: everyone seems to have the need to discuss something from your proposal, mostly in a negative way, why it is not possible. At the end of the process, you often won't even be able to recognize your own idea anymore.'

In the mid-1990s I had a meeting with a group of young Pragmatic managers of the fire brigade. They were talking and complaining about hitting walls in their spontaneous drive to renew the organizational culture. I asked them what they meant when they were talking about a wall. 'We want to renew! But our older colleagues are reluctant to change anything,' they told me. Firstly, we figured out whether the things they wanted to change were the correct focus points, whether they had a point. I know better now, but back then I thought that the participants needed more experience in order to be able to develop an accurate perspective on matters that needed change. The exact opposite turned out to be true: especially members of the younger generations, who are just starting their careers, have proven to be better at making a quick and crystal-clear scan of their surrounding culture, pinpointing which outdated patterns need renewing.

In the years that followed, I used action research to explore in actual organizational life how the obstacles they were talking about came into existence and how they could be tackled. It turned out that an important misunderstanding of members of this young generation was that members of older generations are reluctant to renew outdated organizational routines. This interpretation of the behavior of the oldest generation often seems to stand in the way of renewal. They rarely verified whether this assumption was correct or not. When we discussed this together with the older generation, the complete opposite turned out to be true. The older colleagues did not at all want to curb the enthusiasm of the younger generations. Furthermore, they thought the fact that the younger generation adapted unwillingly to their routines showed spineless and weak behavior. They expected their young, articulate and well-educated colleagues to speak up to their older colleagues. The older colleagues stated that they do not want to discourage their younger colleagues and they genuinely meant it. Nevertheless, young people at most organizations felt curbed in their desire for innovation by their older colleagues. This was not caused by stubbornness. It was caused by the automatic repetition by the seniors of their outdated habits. They seemed to be imprisoned in their outdated routines.

For instance, when the youngest generation indicated what features of the organizational culture needed to be updated, the oldest generation replied by entering into vague discussions on the matter, just like they had always done. These kinds of outdated habits were often overwhelming to these juniors. Members of the younger generation were unable to stand up to this 'tsunami of vague discussions'. They got swept away by it and gave up, because their energy drained away and because of their unspoken perception of their older colleagues: 'You see? They are reluctant to innovate anything.' And this is how young people disappeared into a wave of endless abstract and emotional discussions. When I asked the seniors to stop their discussion and asked the youngest to respond to what happened, the juniors of the youngest generation came 'floating to the surface' again,

In 2007 and in 2012, I attended three European network sessions, two with about forty professionals from the Pragmatic Generation in Brussels and one in Lisbon with about forty professionals from Generation Y. These young professionals from Italy, Spain, Portugal, Hungary, Germany, Denmark, Sweden, Norway and the Netherlands agreed on the top 5 of things that gave them the most energy at work. The differences were found in the way they wanted to communicate about their energizers with their managers from the older generations. In the northern countries, most of them would of course like to talk about their energizers in an open way. In the southern countries, many youngsters experienced a distance towards their senior managers, which seemed to keep them silent and blocked them when it came to communicating openly about their energizers. At that time, there seemed to be more distance and less interaction between generations in the southern countries than in the northern countries.

My generation research in Brazil in 2012 returned very similar findings. Many members of Generation Y said that they could not talk with seniors from the Brazilian Protest Generation: "We do not understand what they say and how they behave and they do not understand us at all." Bearing in mind the rapid growth of the student population at Brazilian universities, growing tension between the oldest generation and the youngest could be forecast.

Fig. 19 Pragmatic Generation in Europe and Brazil

indicating that they wanted a concrete conversation about their proposition. From that moment on, collaboration became more constructive for both the younger generation and the oldest generation. Because members of the older generations have a strong tendency to repeat outdated patterns, endless abstract discussion tends to be a persistent feature at organizations. This does not only put up barriers for younger generations, it also causes energy loss within the older generations, of which they do not seem to be aware. Seniors often simply accepted this energy loss, somehow unwillingly: 'Yes, you are right, but this is how things are here.'

In a number of subsequent experiments in the Netherlands, I asked Pragmatists to try to influence the way of collaboration and communication, instead of going along with the usual methods of working. I gave them maximum influence on the gradual design of the production processes for a large, nationwide project that was organized in order to reach a strategic vision. The leading principle of this experiment was that every move we made in this project needed to generate their work energy. This would enable Pragmatists to stay away from outdated patterns and to develop a pragmatic approach. The characteristics of this pragmatic approach were the following:

a Interactive collaboration, during which actively contributing to the thought process and adding knowledge and insights yielded the best propositions

b Concrete and active collaboration: concrete arrangements, a focus on what needed to be done

c Quick collaboration by doing a number of things at the same time in parallel processes, instead of doing one thing at a time (like the older generations used to do), which reduced the lead time by half.

Members of the Pragmatic Generation appear to prefer to avoid confrontation. Often, we had to stimulate them to express what they experienced in terms of energy loss. Members of this generation do not react in an emotional, primary way, but rather in a rational and secondary way. They feel the need to be understood and to understand what is happening around them. This understanding enables them to spot what they can do to improve a situation, or so they seem to think. Despite the fact that the Pragmatists did not achieve their goal in most cases, they did manage to spread knowledge via networks, beyond the bounds of organizations. With this accomplishment, the members of this generation made a very valuable contribution to the acceleration of the mutual learning process and of sharing knowledge.

Many Dutch Pragmatists have constructed youth networks within bigger companies, governmental institutions and politics. Some were intended to obtain more influence in the existing culture, but most were needed to enable them to share their stories.

In 2014, in collaboration with the Dutch employment agency Timing, I studied the differences between employees with a lower and a higher educational level within a generation. Pragmatists with a lower level of education reported many times that they felt bothered by managers who were trying to think in their place. They may not be as articulate as peers with a higher educational level, but they feel like they are being treated like children. This was very noticeable in their appearance and attitude. It drains away a lot of their work energy, freshness and self-confidence. Sometimes, these members even stop believing that the situation will ever improve. Pragmatists with a higher educational level were taken more seriously, had a stronger tendency to give their opinions and showed more. When they were unhappy about their situation, they started looking for a better job at another company or even started their own firm. They are more likely to take this step than their peers with a lower educational level. When it comes to updating their companies' culture, the focus of Pragmatists with a lower educational level is about the same as their higher educated peers. However, they are still more obedient. An important difference between the two groups of contemporaries is that Pragmatists with a lower educational level have a strong preference for 'doing' things, for constructing concrete things and doing physical labor. The lower educated employees were also more connected to the area where they were born, were less mobile.

Too many employers seem to have the idea that people with a lower educational level have lesser thinking skills, that they are not as smart. This results in a somewhat belittling attitude towards the young people from this genera-tion. Many professionals with a low level of education get caught in this image, make themselves smaller, so to say, and withhold their thoughts. During some experiments, I deliberately adopted the opposite attitude towards the group of lower educated Pragmatists. After about fifteen minutes, they came forward with clear thoughts about their work and about everything that happened around them; it all came floating to the surface. Many professionals with a lower educational level feel like their work is underappreciated. 'Higher educated colleagues can invent all they want, but as long as we do not do the actual work, nothing gets produced or delivered.' Given their repressed reactions, I expect the emancipation of Dutch professionals with a lower educational level – the smart doers – to set in over the years to come.

The Pragmatic Generation and the spirit of the age in the Netherlands, from 1985 to 2000

The members of the Pragmatic Generation spent their second stage of life in the 'commercial' 1980s and 1990s. This may have strengthened this generation's focus on achieving concrete results. Or should we consider this focus to be the Pragmatists' reaction to their idealistic parents, who – in the eyes of the Pragmatists – tend to *talk* more than actually *do* something?

Around the year 1985, the economy started to improve gradually. The number of vacancies increased. Labor participation and the average educational level of women increased sharply. Consequently, unemployment remained rather high. Women of this generation have more influence on their male peers than women of previous generations.

In the Netherlands, the so-called Purple coalition government led by Prime Minister Wim Kok was sworn in in 1994. The idea of a society with the traditional family as its mainstay made way for the idea of a society in which the ability to do things independently and self-determination of the individual were the first matters of importance. This may have influenced the extent to which this generation attaches importance to independence at work. Many parents from the Protest Generation had passed this message on to their children during their upbringing.

The student population grew sharply. In order to cap rising costs, the government cut back on course duration and scholarships.

In 1988, the Dutch national soccer team won the European championships in Germany, sparking a huge party all over the country. Thousands of fans clad in orange lined the canals of Amsterdam during the team's victory parade on a typical Amsterdam canal boat

The advent of information technology (IT) radically changed methods of working and learning at school. More and more low-priced computers hit the market. The Internet made its big breakthrough in the 1990s. The first providers of the dial-up connection made their appearance. After all offices had been equipped with computers, increasing numbers of families also started buying computers. IT companies shot up like mushrooms. Email became a very essential function of the Internet. Many companies and consumers presented themselves via websites. People maintained their social contacts via instant messaging services such as MSN Messenger. A sea of information became accessible via search engines. The Pragmatic Generation is the first generation to have grown up with a computer and the Internet. From this generation onwards, being smart means that you know how and where to find relevant information.

Family reunification meant that immigrant workers from Morocco and Turkey were allowed to bring their immediate family over to the Netherlands to live with them, marking the birth of the multicultural society.
Around 1995, CNN was the world's biggest news network, broadcasting twenty-four hours a day, showing live images

of shocking events. Television brought these images into our living rooms more quickly and realistically than ever. Images of Operation Desert Storm in Iraq (1991). Images of 9/11 (2001). In what way have the young members of the Pragmatic Generation been affected by these impactful images?

The combination of renewed international relations and economic growth brought about a sense of positivity in the Western world during the second half of the 1990s. The year 1997 was an economic peak year.

This sense of positivity, which was accompanied by soaring stock markets, reached its peak around the turn of the century. After the turn of the century, Western countries were hit hard by the bursting of the 'dot-com bubble' that had been allowed to grow on the back of the rapid expansion of the IT industry. In what way did this development affect the members of the Pragmatic Generation?

How will this generation be able to keep their organizations up to date?

Ensuring active support from other generations when it comes to accelerating processes

Whenever I assumed a supporting attitude towards groups of members of the Pragmatic Generation who wanted to renew features of their organizational culture, such as accelerating the process of decision making and making this process more interactive, this actually turned out to be quite an easy thing to do. Members of the Pragmatic Generation often did not receive active support from their experienced colleagues, but neither did they ask for it. This may have been a consequence of the somewhat fundamentally individualistic attitude of this Pragmatic Generation of professionals. These professionals are often quick, analytical thinkers who have a lot of self-confidence on the outside, and who want to take their own responsibility. Older generations tend to think that these well-educated, articulate young people will do fine on their own. This is misleading: these young people will not make it without the support of experienced colleagues. This support is very much appreciated. However, Pragmatists are very critical and they need to have the feeling that support is based on real expertise and that it is given in a concrete way. The Dutch Pragmatists often have bad experiences with this, especially when support is provided in an outdated way: 'I do not need some senior telling me how to handle things, I like to make my own decisions. I would prefer it if he explained to me how he usually handles things. I can learn from that. It might even make me want to improve my own way of working.' But they often consider this attitude as conceited, as a tricky issue. 'I do not want to seem priggish, but I do want to do my job in my own way, a way that works best for *me*. In that way, I feel like I am continually developing myself in my work.'

When young professionals indicate more precisely and more clearly what kind of support they would like to receive, they are able to prevent a misfit between the kind of support that is given, and the kind that is desired. You can do this by explicitly stating that you particularly wish to develop your own methods of working. By making it clear to older colleagues that this is the best and quickest way to learn for *you*. You should also have to keep paying attention, have to stay awake. A senior from the Protest Generation can be

really convinced of the fact that he has found *the* way. He might be able to sell it in such a way that you believe that this is the real truth. You are able to create mutual respect by on the one hand letting it be what it is and saying things such as: 'Gosh, do you really think that?', while adding your own view on the matter to the discussion, for instance by saying, 'Hmm, I think there are always more ways to achieve a goal and that you have to choose the way that fits you best.' This prevents conflict. For seniors, letting go of a persistent attitude can be difficult. I have interviewed many seniors, and found that an open and sincere response is most appreciated. Sometimes, their faces did seem to show the contrary. It may take some time for a senior to react to something. Sometimes, it may even take them a day or longer to respond. It just takes some time for a message to get through to them. Just keep asking for their opinion when you need it. They often do not express it directly: this emanates from a routine, not from obstinacy. To put it briefly: taking charge in communication and striving for a more interactive process of collaboration in a pragmatic way often produces good and surprising results. Because fresh patterns also create vitality and energy in members of the older generations, provided they open themselves up to these updates.

Avoiding adapting to outdated patterns and consciously working in ways that generate work energy

As soon as you and your peers start to detect a decline in work energy and a display of distracted behavior at work, you are probably dealing with outdated patterns. You might experience the tendency to stay in the rhythm of your 'herd', or in a certain situation, and at the same time feel the need to break out of it. You go along with a particular course of events, even though you would like to change it, but you do not know what to do. The question is how to free yourself from this unwanted energy-draining outdated pattern. The first step towards improvement can be to explore with your peers the possibilities of how to break out of this spiral. The next step is to take the lead in this together with your energetic contemporaries. Mentally strong and very energetic people are more able to renew outdated routines in the existing culture. It may also help to share with your older colleagues that you 'are losing a lot of work energy at that moment." Frequently, older colleagues said to be surprised 'that this had not been mentioned before.' I have noticed that with the Pragmatic Generation, the act of sharing these opinions with each other needs to lead to concrete improvements quickly. This is the kind of social innovation that cannot be created by older generations because they have the tendency to repeat their more vague way of communication. Older colleagues can support you, but they cannot do it for you. When members of the Pragmatic Generation are bothered by slowness and vagueness, they need to introduce rapidity and concreteness themselves, in collaboration with their contemporaries. When older colleagues open themselves up to this update and experience the positive effect of this new pattern, they will start to follow in the same direction.

When there is a lot of complaining in your peer group, you first have to turn your complaints around. Complaining is a form of victim behavior. Complaining means suffering. By turning your complaints around, you can start to change your situation into the direction you want to go. When you are complaining about vagueness, you want to go to concreteness. But keep in mind that the temptation by older generations to keep on using outdated patterns can be strong. If you have found a way to bring about rapidity and concreteness, you will need to maintain it for a while, for about as long as it takes to notice that the new pragmatic approach has become integrated into the routines of the older generations. After all, this generates an increased level of work energy for everyone.

At first, bringing about a cultural pattern change like that may give you a feeling of swimming against the tide. You can do this consciously until you start noticing that resistance starts to wane. In the beginning, you need to look for the right direction and the right swimming style as you go along: you will pick up what works for you as you are swimming. Asking explicitly for support and receiving this from responsible managers from the older generation is important, but it does not suffice. It is very important that the older colleagues experience an increase in their energy levels caused by your fresh new social patterns, but this will not suffice either. Once you start to notice that the pragmatic approach has become a new routine, renewal is accomplished. Then it has been integrated into the existing culture. Pragmatists often had the tendency to talk about to accelerate and concretize decision-making processes, however it only happened when they started doing it. Creating a rough image of the pragmatic approach was already sufficient to take the first actions. It works best when Pragmatists pick up how to improve this approach as they go along. You can also think of it as learning how to ride a bicycle. You learn how to ride only by doing it. If you need to cycle against the wind at first, it comes in useful to have enough contemporaries to take turns riding at the front to break the wind. By the way, this might be a typical Dutch example.

Being aware of the resistance towards Generation Y
A couple of times, I noticed that professionals from the Pragmatic Generation – yes, professionals who are only in their thirties – developed a sense of resistance towards the culture renewal that was brought about by the youngest working generation, Y. This surprised me. It seemed to occur mostly with Pragmatists who, involuntarily and subconsciously, had adapted to the outdated patterns of the existing culture the most. This might have caused a kind of premature embitterment. These Pragmatists seem to react strongly to the free and authentic attitude of Yers, while at

the same time – in my opinion – they long to experience this sense of freedom themselves in the form of more independence and responsibility at work. Several times, Pragmatists displayed somewhat irrational, defensive behavior towards members of Generation Y. This came to the fore in questions such as: 'what do you mean flexible working hours, how does that contribute to achieving our goals? How does that improve our work?' Sometimes they were even surprised themselves: 'Gosh, are we already resisting against the behavior of our youngest colleagues?'

It seems like a bad idea to suppress this sense of resistance. There is a good chance that tension will start to mount. This tension will build up and these irritations will be released at the wrong moment. It seems like a better approach to share this sense of resistance openly and directly with the juniors from Generation Y who 'caused' the sense of resistance in the first place and to ask questions to try to understand them. This will create a connection between two generations, provided that Pragmatists make an effort to try to understand the Y juniors' points of view on what they would like to update and try to support Y juniors. Both youngest generations are able to benefit from each other. Generation Yers usually prefer personal and informal contact with colleagues. This can sound somewhat superficial. If Pragmatists really engage with the Y juniors, this may produce the insight that this will improve and accelerate the process of communication and collaboration. Furthermore, Pragmatists' strong sense of reason and Y juniors' strong intuition complement each other very well.

For schools: making use of Pragmatic parents' knowledge on Conscious Generation Z
A number of group conversations with parents from the Pragmatic Generation showed that they, too, know their children very well. They educate their children in a very

conscious way and they are aware of the (vital) characteristics of Generation Z (2000-2015), based on their personal experience. Pragmatic parents who are also teachers should be able to exploit this knowledge in order to establish a type of 'modern' education, which properly suits this new generation of pupils and students. The experiments I ran at sixteen primary schools in the Netherlands showed that the educational methods that correspond best with the pragmatic parenting style, seem to be very effective. Children in schools where teachers showed this style in their interaction with their pupils turned out to become very energetic and lively, and their attitude towards learning was most open-minded. Just to be clear: we also encountered the complete opposite situation. For more information, I would like to refer to the chapter on Generation Z. The first cohorts of Generation Zers started secondary education from 2013. At a few of these secondary schools, I explored – together with teachers from the Pragmatic Generation who were also parents of Generation-Z children – whether they were able to use the knowledge about their own children for the benefit of educational development. These teachers were able to indicate in concrete terms how to make education correspond optimally with this new generation of children/students. It seems as if this relatively cheap and powerful source of information has not been tapped yet. Further research will have to show how this knowledge can be put to optimum use. Further research will also have to show how to share this knowledge with teachers from older generations in an effective way. The time seems right for this, in the Netherlands at least. Teachers of all generations feel a growing need to develop a well-working educational system, by themselves and in collaboration with other teachers. There is a growing sense of resistance against the top-down instructions from the authorities in The Hague and the 'governing bodies'.

7 The Authentic Generation Y as potential pattern innovators

In many countries, people are very interested in the characteristics of the Creative and Authentic Generation Y. There has never been as many studies, articles and books about a generation as there are about these youngsters. Different names are used: Millennials, Bounderless Generation, Internet Generation. What could be the reason for this? Do they symbolize a social evolution that is going on worldwide? By the way, I mentioned this already in the chapter about their parents (Connecting Generation X), almost every company already has plenty of readily available knowledge on Generation Y in their working community. They do not need books and articles to learn more about Generation Y. In fact, learning more about Generation Y by reading books or websites might even be counterproductive. All companies that have questions about Y can harness the real life experience of parents with Generation-Y children and apply this high-quality knowledge to the simple question of what needs to be done or not done to support these Y juniors in their professional and personal development. This will prove beneficial both for the juniors and for their team and their company. In more than two hundred of my Generation X experiments, Xers produced the right answers in a couple of minutes. This also happened in international groups of Xers. These Xers are in the phase of leadership and have the highest impact on the current culture. They just have to do what their own answers tell them.

In young economies, such as Brazil, India, Turkey, South Africa, Kenya, Indonesia, Generation Y is the largest generation. Yet in the Netherlands and many other European countries, it is the smallest working generation.

Strikingly often, Generation Yers see possibilities to handle things differently than usual, and from an evolutionary perspective they are smarter than the older generations and better educated. At most organizations, top-down change and decision-making processes dominate the organizational culture, which is the exact opposite of how Dutch families with members of Generation Y in them work. These outdated top-down patterns curb Yers' creativity. At home, Yers' parents stimulate them to stay themselves and to make their own decisions.

Generation Y juniors have had to deal with the economic crisis amidst soaring youth unemployment across Europe. Were Dutch Generation Y juniors able to remain themselves in such difficult circumstances? Or did or will they adapt to outdated social patterns, just like the two generations before them? In the latter case, the logical result would be early loss of work energy and enthusiasm. And it would spell disaster for many aging companies. Without the updates by Generation Y, a company cannot create the kind of modern culture that is needed to boost its chances of survival in today's fast-changing world!

Compared to previous generations of juniors, Yers are:

- More authentic: they want to feel free to design their own work (content, environment, time) and to create an organization as if it were a second home. At he same time they need feedback from people around them to notice whether what they did out of freedom is really a contribution or not.
- More flexible: they like variation in terms of work, working hours, location and teams.
- More creative: they see many different possibilities to complete daily tasks in a more contemporary way.
- More boundless: they do not care about arguments such as 'that is just the way it works around here.'
- More equal: they do not look up to older people and do not care about hierarchy.
- More spontaneous: they behave in a more informal and open way.
- More open-minded: they are open to different perspectives, open to diversity.
- More skilled in the use of social media and exploiting the advantages of social media.

Point of particular interest: It is important for Y juniors to not start to adapt their behavior to outdated features of the organizational culture, such as out of a kind of fear of being kicked out or staying unemployed. Will this generation be the third in a row, in the Netherlands and other European countries, to adapt its behavior to outdated patterns in organizational cultures? This would be a disaster for our socio-economic and ecological development and for the vitality of our working communities.

Generation Y juniors are more than welcome at most Dutch organizations. Aging organizations in particular need the revitalizing influence of this youngest working generation in order to stay up to date. However, Generation Y is entering the workforce in small numbers, and it will stay the smallest generation. The first cohorts of this generation started working for governmental institutions and in the business world as juniors around 2008. An increasing number of seniors have discovered that they click witthese youngsters and are happy to support this generation. More

and more parents from Generation X are starting to realize that they need to align their behavior as managers or colleagues of Generation Yers with their parenting behavior at home: informal, open-minded and equal. However, this seems to be easier said than done.

In collaboration with Marieke Grondstra and Studelta (www.studelta.nl), I organized two field trips with a group of members of Generation Y. The purpose of this experiment was for the Yers to observe the typical behavior of all working generations. During this experiment, the group of Yers observed the other generations, while these generations were working on a top five of 'energizers' and 'energy killers' at work. The Generation Y groups also reflected on their own working methods. This resulted in the following observations and reactions by the members of Generation Y. The following is a brief recap and uses their own words.
'In our Y group, everyone talks at the same time. It looks rather chaotic. In some sort of strange way, we are able to put our first important energizers down on paper. At high speed, two bouncy Y juniors manage to scribble everyone's thoughts down on a flipchart. Our meeting seems to lack any type of system. Nobody seems to care about that though. Everyone shows great enthusiasm for other people's personal stories and experiences. We ask each other many questions. We're having frank, heart-to-heart conversations about each other's successes and slipups. These conversations make it clear that routine and stagnation are important causes of complete decay. The consequences of this can be terrible, especially when this happens in a first job. We don't have any frame of reference yet. We don't have any previous experience with other organizations and if you're really out of luck, your friends are in the exact same boat. There is a risk that you start to get used to the fact that you're losing a huge amount of energy during your work.'
'Mutual connection turns out to be of great importance

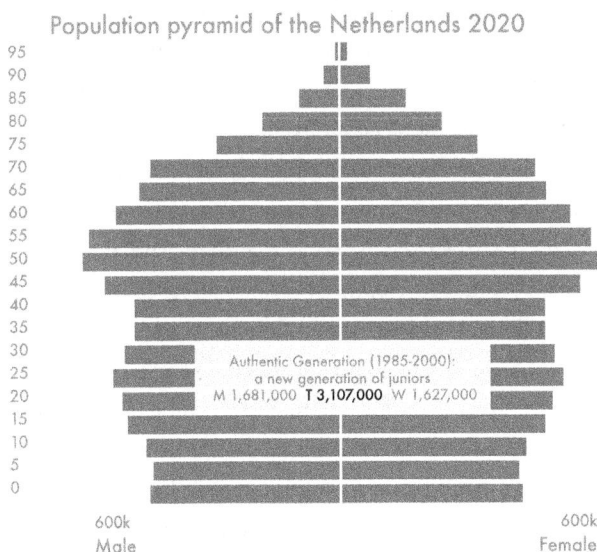

Population pyramid of the Netherlands 2020

Authentic Generation (1985-2000):
a new generation of juniors
M 1,681,000 T 3,107,000 W 1,627,000

600k
Male

600k
Female

Fig. 19 The Dutch population pyramid and the Authentic Generation Y in 2020

to us. We need this in order to experience a kind of team spirit and to be more energetic at work. It is not until we are completely aware of our strengths and of what we've got to offer in an organization, that we will be able to stir up and to renew our working environment. We are the inventors of a whole new phenomenon: the quarter-life crisis. We have found out rather quickly that the reality of working life and organizational cultures doesn't match our naïve idea of the ideal working environment. Our upbringing and the educational system prepared us for a pliant world. However, no one ever told us about the reality that many companies have dominating habits and routines that are very different from ours. This reality differs greatly from our expectations. This is a shocking – sometimes even frightening – realization. Sometimes, this realization is so intense that we are not able to cope with our emotions – with which we seem to be more in touch than any other generation – and we end up in an emotional crisis. Especially so in these times of job scarcity. Sometimes, we seem to have no other choice than to adapt ourselves to the often sluggish and impersonal structures we call organizations. Our grandparents built these organizations. I'm sure they did their best at the time, but do you agree with me when I say that organizational routines could become much better, much quicker, much easier and, especially, much more fun? All those layers and obstacles and formalities... It's enough to drive you up the wall! Surely, it must be driving our older colleagues crazy too. But they just don't realize it anymore... that is the really frightening thing.'

'Bureaucracy? A 9-to-5 mentality? What kind of strange concepts are these? You're supposed to do something because you like doing it, right? That's when you are at your best. You don't need any strict timeframe dictated by managers to be at your best. While we are working, we want to be able to determine our own working hours. Sometimes, our minds and bodies function better in the evening than in the morning.'

'We're also bothered by the whole "yes, but..." mentality. Instead of stimulating a creative way of thinking, all our refreshing plans are torpedoed way before we even get the chance to prove that our ideas are worth listening to. Please, instead of "yes, but...," let's say: "Yeah, let's do it!" Another problem is the lack of confidence in our generation. Yes, we are young, and yes we don't have much experience yet. But that only means that we are able to offer a different, fresh view on outdated problems. Set us free and we start thinking outside the box. Lock us in and we will walk in the same old goose steps as everybody else at the organization. It's either that, or running away as fast as possible and trying to find a place where we feel at home and appreciated. We are more skilled than any other generation when it comes to certain matters. The use of social media, for instance.'

'Constantly having someone watching over your shoulder and the loyalty to hierarchy at organizations kill our creativity. The ambiance alone... Carrying out the boss' orders, orders about which the boss has had endless conversations with his colleagues during their never-ending meetings, and which he thought and thought and thought about... But don't you think for one second that he ever consulted members of younger generations about his decisions. We feel stalemated when someone tells us exactly what to do and how to do it. Our creativity and authenticity are killed by endless protocols, job descriptions, performance reviews, evaluation reviews, personal development reviews, progress reviews, exit interviews, positions, status classifications... phew.'

'We want to be able to be ourselves, and we need our older colleagues to support this and to give us some elbow room. Our parents have always encouraged us to be ourselves; it is deeply embedded in our genes. It feels like getting lost when we don't. As soon as someone starts inhibiting our candid individualities, we clam up. Forcing us to be some kind of non-entity? We don't see that happening any time soon. We'd rather leave to travel around the world, or switch to a completely different industry, or start our own business, somewhere in the world. We chase our dreams, more so than previous generations, however unrealistic or far-fetched our dreams may seem initially.'

'We feel great enthusiasm for positive-minded colleagues who speak of their job and other things in life with passion and an open mind. We want our colleagues to be honest. We want them to stand beside us and to give us advice and assistance. We love to work in an informal atmosphere in which people can laugh with each other and focus mostly on what we are doing *right* and don't just complain about what is going *wrong*. To us, teamwork and collaboration on an equal footing are established when every team member does something they are good at. There needs to be space for creativity and everyone should be able to be involved when it comes to decision making. We like listening to people who are authentic and passionate. People who have valuable life lessons to teach us, based on their personal experience.'

'During these journeYs – yes: with a capital Y – we discovered something very important; something we hadn't expected. We felt a strong connection between us and... yes, the baby boomers (1940-1955, also known as the Protest Generation in the Netherlands). They felt the exact same connection towards our generation. They were much more open towards us than towards other generations, or so they say. They consider our generation to be the rescuing generation that will bring all the changes that are important now, like they did in the 1960s and 1970s. The question is whether we are already able to do so. We think it is really awesome that they look at us that way. They are more than willing to help us. The uninhibited idealism that we share produced a sense of fraternization on the spot. We realize that these skillful baby boomers have considerable knowledge and experience to share with us. This can come in handy for us. It was exactly this unabashed and spontaneous behavior that made these "Protesters" fall in love with us instantly. They

see us as young, real idealists who want to change the world around them. This love is completely mutual.'

In May 2013, the Dutch national youth council asked me to participate in a project of the Social and Economic Council of the Netherlands, in which groups of young people tried to solve the problem of growing youth unemployment. It struck me that these juniors did not put any blame on the government. Instead, they explored possibilities in terms of what they could do themselves to improve the situation.

In collaboration with the Dutch employment agency Timing, I studied the differences between professionals from this generation with a higher educational level and professionals with a lower educational level. Generation Yers with a lower educational level have a greater need for structure and clarity, albeit with respect to things they are passionate about. People with a lower educational level and people with a higher educational level both have similar sources of work energy. They have a similar preference for images, personal contact and a positive open work atmosphere. They set great store by equal, personal and open collaboration, in which people focus on what they CAN do, instead of what they CAN NOT do.

At home, Dutch Y juniors have coaching parents, parents who spend twice as much time with their children as parents from the previous generation did. Many companies have organized meetings to explore ways to attract Y juniors. Never did newspapers, magazines and books publish more articles on one particular generation than they are doing nowadays. Optimists speak of 'smart and creative juniors, who are very familiar with the art of multitasking and who are very skilled in the use of social media.' Pessimists speak of impudent, selfish young people, who are easily distracted and who blurt out every single thought that pops into their head. People who display boundless behavior and who are tied up with their mobile phones.

Dutch Y juniors were confronted with a deep economic crisis

Millennials are lazy (The Guardian, March 7, 2016)
Millennials are accused of being lazy, self-involved, cosseted, politically apathetic narcissists, who aren't able to function without a smartphone and who live in a state of perpetual adolescence, incapable of commitment.

Y job hoppers (Small business-Big impact, May 27, 2014)
More than any other generation, Gen Y is made up of job hoppers. The U.S. Bureau of Labor Statistics reports that the average tenure of a millennial in a position is a mere 4.4 years. Perhaps the reason Millennials are jumping from company to company is because organizations aren't keyed into the perks these young workers want the most.

Y very marketing-conscious (Frankwatching, June 25, 2012)
Generation Y is the most marketing-conscious generation ever. Worldwide, Y's influence on society will be of much more importance than the largely documented influence of the baby boomers. What is it that drives this capricious generation and how are large, world-famous brands going to reach these young people?

Young employees have a horror of hierarchy (HR praktijk, February 4, 2011)
Young employees have difficulties with hierarchical work structures and they want to be able to make their own decisions as often as possible.

Young generation of IT workers will encounter difficulties in their work (Informatie, December 2010)
The youngest generation of IT workers will encounter problems working in a proper way with Web 2.0 tools and social media. In order to implement the development of a New Way of Working, we need a cultural transformation that many companies are not able to carry out yet.

Fig. 20 Snippets from articles published around the time Dutch Generation Yers entered the workforce.

and high youth unemployment. Up to 2016, it was hard for many of them to find a good job. Most young professionals responded rather laconically. They took an extra year to complete their studies, they went to travel through Australia or Argentina, or they went to do 'some fun project in Vietnam first and thought of what to do next upon their return.'
An increasing number of juniors that did get a job appear to adapt to working methods that they actually consider as being outdated, out of fear for dismissal. They think this is a terrible development, but they say that they do not know how to escape from it. At some companies, this has resulted in cynicism and sometimes even in an upcoming sense of apathy.
At the same time, resistance to unwilling adaptation seems to be growing. In May 2015, a large group of students occupied the *Maagdenhuis* in Amsterdam for a couple of weeks. The *Maagdenhuis* is the headquarters of the board of the University of Amsterdam. In 1969, the same building was occupied by the students of that time (from the Protest Generation), marking the beginning of a democratization drive in society and its institutions. The Y students expressed their resistance against the growing 'cold' business attitude of the university, which they claimed focused on financial results more than on people and their development. Interviews held in 2016 with the key players in the *Maagdenhuis* occupation showed that they were disappointed with the results of their actions. The amount of Dutch Y juniors who are actively searching for change is also growing. Last year, I was invited on several occasions by Y networks at different companies to help them create real change. Y juniors are often more aware of what is happening to them and of what they want than the previous generation of juniors. They share their experiences more and the most energetic Y members keep searching for the right actions.
During the economic crisis, some managers at some companies said it was a relief that 'those youngsters started listening again and started to comply with orders again.' These youngsters were probably afraid of losing their job. I

noticed this fear a couple of times. I do not expect anything good to come from this, neither for these companies nor for these juniors. These companies will lack the refreshing contribution and the juniors will lack a healthy development in their career.

Around 2012, youth unemployment peaked in the Netherlands, reaching over sixteen percent; by 2015, it had dropped to eleven percent. Some experts think that the real percentage is much higher. The official figure is based on part-time jobs. The government hardly had any money to fight unemployment as it was. They appointed a youth unemployment czar, who was tasked with finding ways, together with employers, to decrease youth unemployment.

this problem has now gotten through to employers, juniors and municipalities.

The parents of Yers (usually members of Generation X) are very familiar with this situation. Around 1984, many of them went through a similar period of youth unemployment: 17 percent of juniors were out of a job at the time. This also coincided with an economic crisis. The cause of the crisis that we have to face today is way deeper and more complicated. Some economists call it a system crisis. This means that many of our systems, such as financial systems, economic systems, social systems and other types of systems need to undergo a fundamental transformation. In order to bring this transformation about, organizations urgently need the fresh views and activities of Generation Y.

The Authentic Generation Y; the spirit of the age in their second life phase, from 2000 to 2015

Shortly after the start of the new decade, the old economy was beginning to collapse and a new type of economy arose. Many scientists were talking about a system crisis; many systems seemed to be at the end of their lifecycle. Between 1995 and 2001, many Internet-based companies were founded, commonly referred to as dot-coms. A combination of rapidly increasing stock prices, market confidence that the companies would turn future profits, created a lot of speculation with their stocks. Many investors were willing to overlook traditional metrics. The bubble burst over the 1999–2001 period, as many of these companies went bankrupt.

In 2002, the euro was officially introduced as legal tender in the EU member states that had adopted it. In the same year, Dutch right-wing politician Pim Fortuyn was killed because of his groundbreaking behavior in the political world and on television.

Two years later, in 2004, Dutch film and television icon Theo van Gogh was killed in the streets of Amsterdam. He was known for his radical views and his pungent interview style. This event triggered widespread debate on integration. Both left-wing and right-wing parties pleaded for stricter admission requirements for asylum seekers. The general view was that the integration process for immigrants who were already in the Netherlands needed to be improved. In 2006, the compulsory assimilation exam for immigrants was introduced.

International events that had (some) impact.

2001 9/11: Two hijacked airplanes were flown into the Twin Towers in New York City. A third airplane hit the Pentagon (Washington DC) while a fourth airplane crashed in a field in Pennsylvania. These were terrorist attacks by Al-Qaeda, killing 2,974 people and leaving the world in shock.

2004: A powerful earthquake caused a tsunami in Southeast Asia, leaving 230,000 dead

2007: Credit crisis, U.S. mortgage bond market crashed as the subprime mortgage bubble bursts. The dollar exchange rate fell sharply, it became increasingly difficult to borrow money from banks, and investment was down. This affected the entire world economy. A large number of important banks collapsed or received government bailouts.

2008: Start of the banking crisis. Icelandic banks looked like an attractive proposition for savers, but in 2008, these banks became unable to meet their obligations.

2010: Financial positions of Greece, Spain, Italy and Portugal were unstable: the European Union presented a rescue plan and pledged billions of euros.

2011: A tsunami caused a nuclear disaster in Japan.

Internet has become an indispensable factor in our lives. Electronic money transfers have become a regular thing and the gaming industry is growing spectacularly rapidly. E-commerce has emerged. Facebook, Amazon, eBay and Wikipedia have become household names.

Nanotechnology was introduced. Better understanding of DNA functions has led to applied genetic manipulation and other gen-technological applications.

Public awareness of global warming is increasing, thanks to documentaries such as *An Inconvenient Truth* (2006) and events such as *Live Earth* (2007), both by Al Gore. There is a lot of contradictory reporting on global warming. Sustainability has become a serious subject for debate in the Netherlands.

In the world of sports, a culture of doping was exposed as performance-enhancing substances were found in blood samples of several sportspeople. The hunt for dopers was on. Lance Armstrong, winner of seven consecutive Tours de France, was perhaps the most prominent one to be exposed and stripped of his titles.

A lonesome young man attempted to attack the Dutch Royal Family in Apeldoorn during the celebration of Queen's Day (April 30, 2009, a Dutch national holiday) for reasons that remain unknown to this day. He tried to run his car into the Royal family's bus, but missed. Instead, he drove into the crowd and crashed into an obelisk-shaped monument near Het Loo palace. The attack claimed 8 lives, including the life of the perpetrator.

In 2009, Dutch bank DSB (Dirk Scheringa Bank) went bankrupt after it had been (rightfully) accused of financial malpractice.

Between 2012 and 2015, the Dutch government implemented stern cutbacks. Unemployment went up.

A string of musical talent shows emerged on TV, such as 'The Voice of Holland,' 'The Best Singer Songwriter of the Netherlands' and 'Popstars'.

How did these events and the economic and other crises affect Yers? Did Yers stay optimistic? Between 2005 and 2012, the number of Dutch young entrepreneurs aged between 20 and 29 increased by forty percent. As many as 43,000 new companies were registered in the Dutch trade register in 2010, with about four thousand new entrepreneurs under the age 20.

In our society, the sense of optimism that dominated around the year 2000 has made way for an increased sense of pessimism in 2010. People were not as convinced of the fact that 'everything will be all right' as they were before, and they started to feel insecure about the future. In 2014, we expected to regain a bit of hope. But in 2016, we seem to be slipping into a European political crisis. In 2017, the economic crisis seems to have ended, but other crises seem to be around the corner.

How will this generation be able to keep their organizations up to date?

Generation Yers: be yourself and stay away from outdated patterns!

Sounds easy, but it often turns out to be difficult to do. The subconscious and often subtle pressure from the work environment that forces people to go along with existing patterns can be strong. The experienced, coaching colleague – from the Protest Generation, because Yers seem to 'click' with this generation – might love to support Y juniors to find ways to NOT adapt to the outdated patterns and at the same time keep a positive connection with their colleagues. As I mentioned before, over the past years I have noticed that an increasing number of juniors were involuntarily adapting to outdated ways of collaboration. This was often caused by the recent economic crisis with high youth unemployment and the fear of getting fired. Contracts nowadays are usually temporary ones. Adapting to outdated patterns is bad for the development of these juniors and it creates stag-

nation in the evolution of 'their' teams and organizations. For some companies, this is still a dead end road, literally.

Directing the interaction between older and younger generations

Things will go wrong – i.e. the amount of work energy will decrease – between younger and older generations as soon as the older generations' outdated patterns become dominant out of sheer habit. By becoming aware of the fact that this process is taking place, you will enable yourself to break through these patterns. You can find ways to intervene and to direct the interaction at hand by doing things that energize you. Then you might find the way to renew the outdated patterns at hand.

For example, whenever a heated discussion threatens to arise, you can try to insistently ask for someone's opinion instead of agreeing with the popular points of view or withdrawing yourself from the discussion. Another example: whenever you are fobbed off with the usual 'that is just how we do things here,' you can try to ask your colleagues whether this routine generates any work energy for them and whether there is anyone who actually knows why things are done that way at your organization. Attempt to make it clear to your colleagues that you think you know a way to change and to improve these outdated routines, and that you would like to try out your ideas. Do it and ask your colleagues for support and to join you in your thought process. You will never get permission to go over the boundaries of the existing culture. The reward will come afterwards, as you experience an increase in the level of human energy and vitality, both in yourself and in your older colleagues. You could also make a kind of a joke of it. By asking your older colleagues how long the work-energy-draining routine has been around. Suppose they say something like 'Oh for many years, perhaps even decades.' Then you could respond with 'Really, that long, well then it surely needs an update. Sorry, but if I wouldn't update my cell phone for such a long time, I would have to throw it away. Maybe we do not have to throw this routine away, but let's see how we can update it. I can do it, but I really need your support and feedback. You might feel the difference too.'

Try to break through the habit of only seeing what is going wrong and what possible obstacles are by asking your colleagues about the opportunities they see. It may help if you prearrange a way to react together with your Generation Y contemporaries; make sure that you have an accurate approach prepared on which you can fall back as soon as an outdated pattern arises. It can be useful to think about ways to break through these patterns in advance. Spontaneous flashes of inspiration often form an excellent source for interventions. It may also be helpful to ask your peers this question: 'What will generate the highest possible level of work energy for us in this situation?'

Of course, you could share your energy-draining experiences at work with your peers through social media and ask for energizing suggestions.

Having faith in your own observations

This new generation of juniors is very able to transparently identify the outdated features in the surrounding culture. They only need a short period of work experience at the company. One or two months might be sufficient. I made *Y scans* with groups of members of Generation Y at about sixty different Dutch organizations. A *Y scan* can be best compared to an MRI scan of the existing culture in which outdated patterns and the updates from Generation Y come floating to the surface. The scan takes only one hour and is of very good quality and highly precise: Yers are better able to create a clear image of the fitness or vitality of an organizational culture than any consultancy firm. Y groups produce the scan faster, sharper and cheaper. This is because the youngest generation is most sensitive to outdated routines and at the same time they are carriers of the new-

est updates. Without input from the youngest generation at work, a company cannot become fully up to date. It is dazzling that only very few companies have cottoned on to this.

Forming innovative teams with vital seniors from the Protest Generation

As I mentioned before, strikingly, many Y juniors clicked with the vital seniors from the Protest Generation. The members of the Protest Generation felt the same way about the Y juniors. These groups of seniors and juniors are able to form valuable innovative teams, without excluding others, of course. Whenever I brought the youngest and oldest working generations together, they felt this potency as well. Both the Y juniors and Protest seniors think they can learn a lot from each other while working together. This mutual click, combined with a shared passion for their job, appears to be crucial for productive and innovative collaboration. I assume that such a team, consisting of seniors and juniors, is capable of tackling even the most stubborn problems. However, I have not yet collected any examples that show footage of this potency being brought into action. I showed this potency many times in my master classes by bringing together the three oldest seniors and the three youngest juniors in front of the audience and asking them to talk about what they could learn from each other – it only works well when these groups are willing to look at both sides! Usually, after a couple of minutes, a kind of chemical reaction could be observed, reflecting the so-called click. Everybody could see and feel it.

Leaders from Generation X – most of them are parents of Y children – could be tempted to act the same way at work as they do at home in their X/Y families.

(I would like to refer to the chapter on Generation X in which I already brought up this phenomenon). You can imagine what would happen to your company if Generation

Xers adapt to outdated ways of leading, communicating and cooperating and their children from Generation Y do the same!!! You can also imagine what would happen if both generations did the opposite, did their work in a way that generates great energy for them at work!!!

It would be really very helpful if Xers and Yers acted the same way at work as they do in their private life, at home. Y juniors can help Xers with that if they start communicating in an equal, open and direct way with colleagues from their parents' generation, in the same way as they are used to doing at home. This will help Generation Xers let go of outdated patterns that they have taken over involuntarily. Perhaps, Y juniors need to mind their language a little bit, but in the end, it is all about their fundamental attitude. The outdated patterns that members of Generation X have taken over involuntarily are visible in somewhat introverted, distant, formal and hierarchical behavior. Every time I presented the possibility of copying their typical Generation Y behavior from their home life to their work life, Y juniors' reactions were rather hesitant. Some of the juniors said they did not dare to assume this kind of attitude at work. However, the vast majority of Generation Y said that they would like to make their working environment feel like a second home. This can be achieved by behaving at work as they do at home. Although this may seem simple, in reality it means that they have to step out of or break through an outdated mainstream in the current organizational culture, for survival reasons. When the older generations, including X, openly and actively support Generation Y in doing so, this will make it much easier for the Y juniors.

8 The Conscious Generation Z, children of pragmatic parents

At the moment, Generation Z – the most uninhibited, conscious and media-savvy generation – is the newest generation of Dutch children. The first cohorts are now in secondary education and Generation-Z juniors will move on to higher education or vocational training in a couple of years. Around 2022, the first cohorts will enter (aging) Dutch companies. At this moment (summer of 2017), schools and universities in the Netherlands do not prepare them for work in gradually aging working communities.

Analysis of video recordings of groups of children at sixteen primary schools spread over various regions in the Netherlands has painted the following, provisional picture. This research was carried out in 2012 and 2013, in collaboration with Marieke Smeets of Studelta and with the Now It's our Time team.

We asked the groups, each consisting of about nine ten-year-olds, to draw up a top six of things they find very important in their lives. We also asked the group members to come up with a list of qualities a good teacher needs to have. We asked them to discuss what kind(s) of social media they used or did not use and what they had learned from or taught their (grand)parents. We also recorded the entire process. A team of researchers analyzed these videos to study typical generational behavior. We also asked twelve groups of parents of children from this generation to talk about what they considered important when it comes to the upbringing of their children and in which educational themes they were particularly interested. The following figure sums up the results of this research.

Compared to the members of the generation that preceded them, members of Conscious Generation Z are:

- Even more conscious of themselves and their environment.
- More conscious of (group) processes.
- More open: it is as if all of their senses are wide open to everything that happens around them. Zers are able to observe in a broad, clear and quick way and they are very capable of putting their observations into words.
- More direct and uninhibited: they feel free to say anything that pops into their head and they do not impose anything on the people around them. They feel free and they are well disciplined.
- More spontaneous and intuitive and rational by nature.
- More conscious that love is important.
- More open to collaborating, especially in groups of five. They are taught to work together already in primary school. Whenever I visited these primary schools, everywhere I looked, I saw small groups of children working together. These children are already part of social networks at a very young age.
- More distracted. They have a shorter attention span and they need variation.
- More active as go-getters. Their parents taught them to persevere, even when things do not necessarily go their way.
- More informed about the possibilities and the disadvantages of social media. They usually start using social media at a very young age. Their parents were brought up with computers and therefore know how to set boundaries, using well-founded arguments.
- More busy at an earlier age.
- More skilled at processing information quickly.
- More attached to equality. Z children pay attention to children who cannot keep up with the other children in order to help them out.
- More self-confident. Their parents and their computer screens provide these Z juniors with a lot of positive feedback from a very young age. Z juniors easily find their way in games, social networks and in family life. This makes them very self-confident.

When we asked these Z children to do something that was not intuitively experienced by them as something that

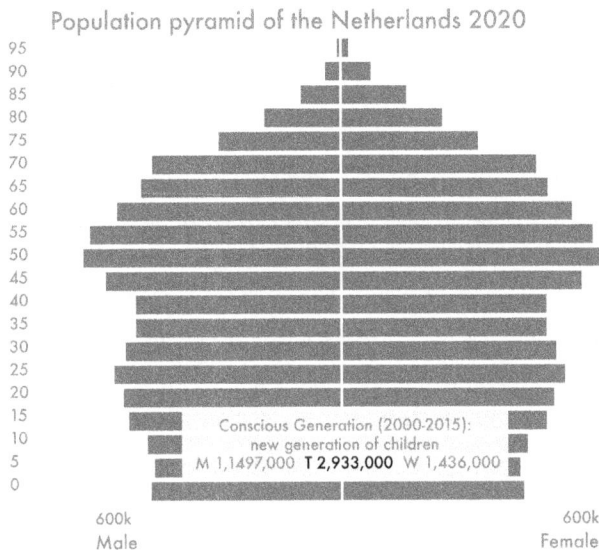

95		
90		
85		
80		
75		
70		
65		
60		
55		
50		
45		
40		
35		
30		
25		
20		
15		
10		
5		
0		

Conscious Generation (2000-2015):
new generation of children
M 1,1497,000 T 2,933,000 W 1,436,000

600k
Male

600k
Female

Fig. 22 The Dutch population pyramid and the Conscious Generation Z in 2020

made sense to them, they just did not move. Well, to be precise, they created chaos in that situation. They just did not move in the direction that we had planned. They were not refusing or protesting or expressing negative emotions towards us; they just seemed to be confused and did not go along with what we asked them to do. However, when we gave them a group task that they loved, they moved forward very quickly with an outburst of energy and great fun. When the group was bigger than five – the size of the group they were used to work with – at first there was a kind of chaos, but within a few minutes they found their way and finished the task very quickly. In 95 percent of the tasks, the girls were the ones leading the group. During the task, one of the girls led the group for a couple of minutes, until she did not know what to do, and another girl took over the leading position, again for a couple of minutes, until she did not know what to do, started laughing about that, and another girl took over.

Point of particular interest: It is very likely that this generation will 'produce' many female leaders. In 95% of the tasks we assigned to the groups of children – every group was assigned three tasks – girls led the process. Further research will show if this is a forerunner of a strong increase in female leadership. This, in turn, leads to the question of whether boys will be able to stay strong amid this development or not. How boys are going to be able to develop their own strength in an increasingly feminine culture (Hofstede, 2001; Bontekoning 2007, 2014) can become an important question. On the whole, girls at all schools were more energetic than boys.

I am calling this picture 'provisional' because of the fact that we do not know how the behavior we saw will continue to be typical of this generation of boys and girls once they hit adolescence. Generally, patterns in values are assumed to stabilize around the twelfth year of life (Hofstede 2001; Oppenhuisen, 2000). After children have reached this age, it will be difficult for them to alter their values. It is likely that this applies to the typical behavior of a generation as well. This means that the generational foundation starts to take a rather definite shape at the end of the stage of childhood, via the upbringing of a child and interaction with peers and other educators, such as their teachers. After this, they will build on and develop from this foundation.

Another experience supporting the claim that generational and personal characteristics stabilize at the end of the first life phase is one I have had personally on several occasions, and which I have shared with many of my peers. Whenever I meet peers from my school days at a reunion, people I haven't seen for years, I recognize the way they act, the way they walk and talk, the way they smile and make jokes or have stayed quite serious people. Their behavior is very similar to what their behavior was when they were around fifteen years old. The most important change is their life and work experience, which is reflected in their attitude, eyes and face.

But their foundation, their basic behavior and value pattern seems to be about the same. Of course, there are exceptions, peers that went through a personal crisis that has shaken their foundation in a way that has changed them on certain points.

Around 2022, the first members of Generation Z will enter the Dutch workforce. It will be the smallest working generation. Compared to the current situation, many companies will have an even greater number of seniors in their employ by then.

In June 2013, I took part in a study by the young research collective Now It's our Time (NioT). We studied how Dutch children (aged between five and sixteen) perceive education and learning. In 2012, NioT had run a study into how children aged between five and fifteen perceived their environment. I have summarized the results of these studies in the following paragraphs.

In general

Children have many options nowadays. They are able to express their own opinion online and they learn to look at things from different points of view. Some children experience the large number of options as too many. They are used to learning together. To children, school is a place to meet their peers. Most of what they learn in life is learned here. They like to talk about life to each other. They learn from those conversations. Until their twelfth year of life, Generation Zers' parents are the most important factors in their lives. From that time on, friends become (more and more) important. Their choices in life depend on their friends and on what peers on social media tell them. Boys set great store by facts, details and humor. Girls feel the need to establish social relationships.

Zers do not consider heroes to be role models; their heroes are people who are really good at something. The children hardly mentioned any favorite brands. They get to decide what they want to wear for themselves. One fifth of the children between twelve and fifteen years old receive a clothing allowance from their parents.

At home and with their Pragmatic parents

The Dutch Pragmatic, networking parents of the Conscious Generation Z are accustomed to the interactive exchange of educational questions. They discover what does and does not work along the way. They consciously decide that they want to have children, and at what age they would like to have them. They support their children in being aware of what happens around them. Pragmatic parents explain things to their children, such as when there is a car accident in front of them or something else that attracts the child's attention. They spend 'quality time' with their children, which means that for a couple of hours every week they adapt to the rhythm of their children, doing what the children want to do, such as going shopping together. Pragmatic parents also encourage their children to do what they are good at.

Many Dutch Pragmatic parents are searching for non-hierarchical ways to set boundaries for their uninhibited children. Among other things, they want to set boundaries for the use of social media. Parents are of the opinion that schools should focus on fostering their children's independence, as well as respect and perseverance. In their view, children's upbringing should be about love, respect, independence and confidence. This new generation of children generally has vital grandparents, predominantly from the Protest Generation. I would still like to find out in what way this has affected the development of these children. It seems like many of these grandparents see their grandchildren on a regular basis. Grandchildren teach their grandparents how to use social media. This contact appears to take place in a remarkably straightforward and equal way; Z children do not consider their grandparents to be superior to them.

These are parents who pay extremely close attention to a child's or children's experiences and problems, particularly at educational institutions. Helicopter parents are so named because, like helicopters, they hover overhead, overseeing their child's life. Many Dutch children have a mobile phone and can call their parents any time, to solve a problem or to say that they arrived safely at school. The other way around parents can call their children to ask how they are doing. Or they communicate by means of WhatsApp. Some families have a family WhatsApp group.

Some studies have shown that overprotective, overbearing or over-controlling parents can cause long-term mental health problems for their offspring. The description of these mental health problems may possibly be lifelong and its impact comparable in scale to individuals who have suffered bereavement, according to University College London. According to the Medical Research Council "psychological control can limit a child's independence and leave them less able to regulate their own behavior."

Dr. Deborah Gilboa, founder of AskDoctorG.com, offers this advice: "As parents, we have a very difficult job. We need to keep one eye on our children now – their stressors, strengths, emotions – and one eye on the adults we are trying to educate. Getting them from here to there involves some suffering, for our kids as well as for us. In practical terms, this means letting children struggle, allowing them to be disappointed, and when failure occurs, helping them to work through it. It means letting your children do tasks that they are physically and mentally capable of doing. Remembering to look for opportunities to take one step back from solving our child's problems will help us build the reliant, self-confident kids we need."

Sources: Wikipedia and www.parents.com

Fig. 23 Parents and their protective attitude towards Generation-Z children

Many Dutch Z children are of the opinion that their parents are too busy too often. Their parents are stressed out and grouchy too often. They lack time to act spontaneously and to have a good conversation with their children. They also fight too much. Z children hate quarrelling. They appreciate receiving support from their parents. They also think that their parents need to set boundaries. Twenty-five percent of children from Generation Z have divorced parents. More than fifty percent of Generation-Z children eat with their parents at home every day of the week. Thirty percent of them eat together with their parents five or six days per week. French fries and pancakes are Z children's favorite dishes; the children associate this food with a celebration. They think a healthy diet is important as well. Being healthy is important to them, because it makes you look and feel good. Spending time together and doing things together in their family life, at school and when they are practicing sports is very important for them. On average, they exercise 4.9 days a week, for thirty minutes per day. This includes cycling to school, playing outside and practicing sports.

Life at school

The atmosphere at school needs to be fun and cozy. A teacher is the most important factor. Z children are put off by uncertainty about the future and pressure from their parents and/or school to work hard. What may help in stimulating these children is adding practical elements and topical subjects to classes and making sure that lessons are diverse and let children work together in groups. Dutch Z children want to be considered as individuals, they want to discover their strengths and to develop their talents. Social pressure from peers encourages them to do the best they can. Z children work hard for things they are passionate about and tend to ignore things in which they are not interested. In general, they are pleased with their school and their teachers, but some things really need some improvement. Zers feel that quality education and basic subjects such as mathematics and reading and writing are important for their future. They say they need these subjects in order to find a good job and to make money so they will be able to take care of their own family later in life. Creative subjects and physical education teach them important skills, such as harmoniously working and communicating together. It also gives them self-confidence. They want to know why they are taught something and what the material's practical purpose is. They need IT lessons. At the moment, they are learning how to work with IT at home; they are taught IT skills by their brothers, sisters and friends. They mostly use their digital devices at home. Schools often have outdated digital aids or they do not have any at all. Children often know more about IT than their teachers. Whenever Z children are taught something about the use of Internet, it mostly concerns the possible dangers involved. They learn via paper books, interactive whiteboards and laptops – most likely because very few schools know how to use digital aids as a means of learning in an effective way or schools have limited budgets. Z children think that the educational system could be more challenging, by making use of new techniques and methods. Making use of iPads can make classes more fun and exciting and it would add some variation. Z children want more creative subjects and they want to be active together. Teachers do not need to be 'cool,' but they do need to be inspiring. Teachers need to offer context and answers to questions such as 'Why am I learning this?' They want to know what the practical purpose is of whatever they are taught. Teachers need to add structure to learning processes, preferably using humor and passion. Z children also want to know what teachers have to offer them. They need to be authentic. The most important thing to Z children is to have good rapport with their teacher. Since they have so many options to choose from, they consider it to be very important to have someone to talk to about important topics, such as who they are, what they want to achieve in life and how they are supposed to accomplish their goals. Z children think that the educational system should focus more on:

- Ways to look up relevant information and ways to filter and process all of this information.
- Better teaching methods.
- Personal contact and learning in a practical way, for example by working together with peers.
- Learning by means of digital aids, such as a tablet, laptop or smartphone.

IT, books and TV

Generation Zers are being brought up in a digital age. They use Google, WhatsApp, Twitter, Instagram and Snapchat and they find email old-fashioned. Children between the ages of six and eleven think it is 'cool' to have a lot of digital friends: on average, they have between one hundred and two hundred of them. Older children prefer quality to quantity. Fifty percent of Z children own a computer. Usually, these are the oldest children of the family. The younger children in particular like to read. They especially like the books from the Dutch *Hoe Overleef Ik* (How do I survive...) series. These books are about Rosa, a teenage girl who has reached puberty and encounters all kinds of teenage problems and adventures. Older children have less time to read and prefer comic books. Their favorite weekly comic book is still Donald Duck (exists only in the Netherlands as a magazine for young children).

Almost fifty percent of the older children and 34 percent of the younger children watch TV one to two hours per day. Their favorite channels include the informative public broadcasting channels *Nederland 3, Discovery Channel, National Geographic* and *Disney XD*. After children reach the age of eleven, they start watching channels such as MTV. Television programs teach Dutch children how to speak English. These channels enable children to learn about the world around them, and to learn that there are many more countries and other people in the world.

About sixty percent of the younger Z children own a mobile

phone. Almost one hundred percent of the older children own a mobile phone. They use their phones especially to play games, to use WhatsApp or to use other apps as a way to get in touch with their parents. Obviously, they have Internet access. About forty percent of these children use the Internet between one or two hours per day, twenty-one percent use the Internet between three and four hours per day. Young children use the Internet the most, whereas older children use it the least. Children between the ages of twelve and sixteen use the Internet two to three hours per day; particularly to play games, to watch funny videos on YouTube, to use social media or to help them with their homework. About sixty percent of these children use social media one to two hours per day.

Given that digital aids will keep on being improved, I expect that more and more schools will start to make use of the knowledge that (some) children have of these modern developments. Students and teachers will be learning more from other students. The teacher's role will become more one of 'a coach of the learning processes.'

The spirit of the age in the Netherlands from 2015 to 2030

By now (2017), the economic crisis has indeed ended in the Netherlands, but other crises are popping up: Brexit and EU cooperation; European migrant crisis; increasing awareness of the environmental crisis; leadership crisis in politics. The extent to which we will get through these crises will most likely mark the spirit of the next age. Will the social evolution that was started by new generations in their different life stages continue? Or will we get stuck in (too many) outdated patterns? Will the evolution continue or will these crises result in a revolution?

The phenomenon of population aging in the Netherlands will peak around the year 2035 and it will gradually subside from then on. There is no getting away from this. Howev-

er, it is less easy to predict the degree to which population aging will lead to outdated organizations. Generation Z will be the newest generation to start working between 2023 and 2038; the same period as when the phenomenon of population aging will reach its peak.

Our society will become more and more multicultural. Amsterdam is home to people from around 180 countries. Age diversity at organizations will increase, because of the fact that the older generations will work longer. It is very likely that macho behavior will fall by the wayside and that feminine behavior will take over. It is possible that these two types of behavior will mix in a way that we cannot yet foresee. The power of big institutions and authorities in the Netherlands will most likely shift towards professionals and individuals in varying networks. Power will no longer be based on hierarchy; it will be taken over by people with current knowledge and expertise and by networks that revolve around this expertise. Leadership will remain of great importance and it will shift towards a more coaching, facilitating, connecting and directing management style. More and more women will occupy positions of leadership in the years to come.

For more information on the spirit of the age ahead of us, I would like to refer to the next chapter about social evolution.

The generational effort of the Conscious Generation Z

Responsibility for making a generational effort in the years to come lies mostly with parents, teachers and other educators. The first cohorts of Generation Z entered secondary education around 2014. It is most likely that the educational system needs to be attuned to this new generation, in order to support its optimum development. The right course of action should be developed in collaboration with the parents of this generation, as I mentioned before when I discussed the Pragmatic Generation. Pragmatic parents, people who are already present at schools as teachers, are able to play an important part in this process. They know this new generation very well, and they have a sound grasp of the current educational system. These teachers/parents of Z children are well placed to indicate which improvements are needed to better align the Dutch educational systems with their children.

The current situation shows that the areas for improvement also seem to have to do with developing self-discipline and resisting temptations that can lead, among other things, to putting on weight, obesity, or excessive use of social media. The educational level has kept on increasing continuously for previous generations, but this rise seems to come to an end, at least for boys in the Netherlands. Boys of the next generation are more likely to end up with a lower education level than their fathers. Perhaps, the contribution that modern education is able to offer to the personal and professional development of people has past its peak. Many educational institutions are aware of this process. These institutions are experimenting with new educational formats. Today, the best lectures at the world's best universities are published online. The teacher's role is likely to shift towards one of counselor in children's learning processes.

In the context of this development, a report entitled 'The Learning Curve 2012' (Pearson, 2013) makes for a very interesting read. It is a benchmark study on educational efforts and results, carried out in fifty countries, spread over all continents. Among the participating countries were the following: the Netherlands, Finland, South Korea, Japan, Australia, Poland, Russia, Brazil, the United States, Mexico and Argentina. Governments of many of these countries acknowledge and recognize a connection between the quality of knowledge and skills young people acquire thanks to the educational system and the socio-economic development of a country in the long term. This has led to many more studies all searching for factors that stimulate excellent academic records. These accomplishments contribute to the development of highly qualified working communities. I will summarize the conclusions of these studies. Despite the fact that an enormous amount of data has been collected and processed, the 'holy grail' has not yet been found. Neither have these studies found a direct route to excellent academic performance. There is a possibility that this route simply does not exist; it varies from culture to culture. The most important factor in the quest for excellent education is the extent to which education and teachers are supported and appreciated consistently and permanently by the surrounding culture in the long term. I will summarize some of the other research results:

1 Competent teachers play an important part, but it is not possible to draw up a universal profile of the perfect teacher, nor is it possible to describe a way to develop a perfect teacher.

2 Successful schools:
   a) attract the best teachers
   b) support their teachers by offering them relevant training
   c) make sure teachers have a status that is equal, compared to other professions
   d) set clear and transparent goals that teachers both want (and are able) to accomplish.
   Successful schools do not treat teachers as technical engineers in a big educational machine.

3 What works well is to offer parents clear information, which can help them in choosing the right school for their children.

4 Stimulating quality education occurs when school boards involve parents in the process of educational development.

5 The best schools teach their students future-proof skills. These schools attune their programs to what is needed in the future; they prepare their students for the jobs of the future with educational programs that are attuned to this

expectation. Many jobs that are important today will no longer exist in about twenty years.

'The future belongs to the young' can be interpreted rather literally. Every new generation of children carries the future along within them, in the new social patterns that they bring forward. In the Netherlands and in most of the other European countries, their future will be set in a strongly aged society. Older generations will be in the majority; up to 2035 there will be more seniors in the Netherlands than ever before. From a positive viewpoint, this means a growing amount of expertise available to juniors. From a negative viewpoint, this means a risk of being overwhelmed by outdated routines.

It will become important for these juniors to be prepared for work in aging teams and at aging companies, and to learn how to benefit from the amount of expertise around them, as well as how to escape outdated routines and how to update these patterns. Many seniors will be able to actively support the development of this new youngest generation at work. The degree to which they actually show their support will determine whether this new generation of children will flourish or not. Aside from that, there are the effects of the efforts made by the children themselves. Part of these processes will take place across the boundaries of the culture that has been built up by older generations over the years. When older generations give juniors free rein, and if they support them actively, this will stimulate our social evolution. This evolution will keep the social system that they are a part of vital and up to date, which is a mutual interest.

9 Differences between generations in terms of social media use

When we use the term 'social media', this includes all digital tools that people use for their mutual communication via the Internet. Social networks such as WhatsApp, Facebook, YouTube, Snapchat, LinkedIn and Instagram are currently the most popular media. Over the past two years, the popularity of Facebook and WhatsApp has increased slightly, the number of users of YouTube and LinkedIn has increased by about 31 % and Instagram by 50 %. Use of Foursquare and Tumblr has decreased about 13 %. WeChat and Snapchat are becoming very popular in the Netherlands. Tumblr, Foursquare and Twitter are becoming less popular. The results of a study on the use of social media (*Newcom Sociale Media Onderzoek Nederland*, 2017) that was recently carried out showed that this is a phenomenon that occurs in all generations that have been studied.

- Social media have been integrated into our daily lives. About eight in ten people in the Netherlands use social media on a daily basis

- Social media are no longer a hype. They now belong to the established communication channels
- Many people are less trusting of social media, they are afraid of misuse of their data; in the age category of 15-19, 27 percent trusts social media and in the age category of 40-64, 11 percent trusts social media. Trusting social media will become an important issue over the coming years
- Two-thirds of the people of over fifty years old use social media; the number of 50+ users of Facebook, WhatsApp and Instagram will increase gradually over the coming years
- Many people in the Netherlands are worried about their privacy. Yet, despite this anxiety, they use social media more frequently
- Number of daily users of different social media in the Netherlands (2015):
  Facebook 6.6 million; Google+ 1.3; YouTube 1.2 million; Twitter 1 million; LinkedIn 0.4.

Dutch users of social media

Users (milion)	Daily (1.000)	Media	Change (%)	15-19 (%)	20-30 (%)	40-65 (%)	65-79 (%)	80+ (%)
2.6	871	TWITTER	-0	23	25	19	10	8
2.4	381	PINTEREST	14	16	25	19	11	4
1.9	960	SNAPCHAT	77	67	25	4	1	0
0.4	101	TUMBLER	-11					
0.1	63	WECHAT	40					
0.1	46	FOURSQUARE	-16					
10.9	7.800	WHATSAPP	11	96	93	85	61	36
10.4	7.500	FACEBOOK	10	80	89	77	68	61
7.5	1.700	YOUTUBE	31	86	72	51	38	26
4.3	400	LINKEDIN	33	13	47	35	15	7
3.2	1.500	INSTAGRAM	50	66	36	17	7	3

Fig. 24 Differences in daily use of social media by age groups

Internet skills

Alexander van Deursen, professor at the department of Media, Communication and Organization of the University of Twente, the Netherlands, obtained his doctorate degree with a dissertation on different levels of Internet skills among the Dutch population. He distinguished two types of skills.
- Strategic skills: skillfully finding the right information
- Operational skills: the ability to use social media

He also distinguishes a 'digi-consciousness'. This is the extent to which people are conscious of the possibilities of social media. According to Van Deursen, the age of a person affects the strategic Internet skills directly and in a positive way. Older people have more experience recognizing the relevance of certain information. They search and select information in the same way as they have always done, regardless of whether they are using old or new media. Older people are better able to recognize relevant search results, because they are able to judge and compare them in a more critical way. They have a better overview and they are good at planning and classifying information. As young people's brains have not matured yet, they are not yet able to execute strategic tasks. However, when it comes to understanding menu structures on websites, links and files, young people are more skilled than older people. Young people are very curious, they are open to new ideas and they try out new social media immediately. They discover the possibilities of social media as they go along and this is how they develop their operational skills so quickly. Many children nowadays play games on a smartphone, iPad or tablet before they are even able to speak.

The influence of social media on behavior

The strong rise of social media also leads to debates on the risks it carries for the youngest generations. Sherry Turkle, Abby Rockefeller Mauzé Professor of the Social Studies of Science and Technology at the famous Massachusetts Institute of Technology, wishes to prime the debate on how we want to live side by side with technology. Has technology become a sort of 'phantom part of our bodies'? Have we become so used to the possibility of being able to communicate via social media at all times and places, that we cannot imagine our lives without it?

Sabina Meiling, who co-wrote this chapter with me, once asked eight different groups of first-year students to go offline for one hour. After the experiment, she listed the experiences. The responses she collected from the students included the following:
- 'I really want to hold something in my hand, I want to check my messages and email'
- 'I feel left-out when I am not online'
- 'I am better able to focus when I have Internet to hand'
- 'I want to be able to look up and re-read matters we discussed in class right away'
- 'I think life is boring without the Internet'

These results suggest these students fight against a certain emotional dependency towards their electronic device and that the students have an urgent need for a connection with other people and a quick access to information. These new habits seem to become deeply embedded in the nature of this generation.

In her book, Turkle paints a picture of the way in which the use of social media influences the behavior and the identity of the members of Generation Y's youngest age categories. These juniors tell her that they are constantly busy updating their Facebook page. They need to look good in their profile picture; their music preferences and other interests need to be filled in correctly. Insecurity is an important and – according to Turkle – unhealthy motive to spend so much time on your (online) image. She also brings up the phenomenon of multitasking for discussion. When you are multitasking, the neurotransmitter dopamine is released in your brain, which makes you feel better. This leads to more multitasking. According to Sherry Turkle, teachers and students need to regain the art of 'unit asking': learning how to focus on one single task at a time.

A very interesting experiment, carried out by Mathieu Weggeman, professor of innovation management at Eindhoven University of Technology, throws some doubt upon Turkle's propositions. Weggeman studied the effects of multitasking on academic performance and the satisfaction of his students about his university classes by carrying out an experiment with his own students. During a class on innovation management, he decided to start innovating his own lectures, completely in character with Generation Y's need for renewal. He first organized a short series of classes in the same way as he had always done, spreading three lectures out over three weeks. In the first week of his experiment, he gave an 'old-fashioned, yet respectable' lecture on stage-gate processes. During the second class, he showed a movie on the Apollo 13 mission. This movie showed how things can go wrong because of a stage-gate error. In the third week, the students were asked to work together on a real case of global science-based company DSM. Afterwards, students had to take a test on the content of all three lectures. They achieved an average score of 7.2 out of 10. Inspired by Generation Y, Weggeman then decided to organize all three lectures at once. He combined all three lectures, according to the principal of 'parallel processing'. During a one-and-a-half-hour class, Weggeman showed the presentation of the first lecture, while playing the movie on the Apollo 13 mission with sound and subtitles on a loop at the same time. And the students also worked on the tough DSM case at the same time.

At the end of this multitasking class, they took the same test as they took after the normal classes. They managed an average score of 6.9 out of 10. Weggeman's tentative con-clusion was that multitasking goes at the expense of quality. The score dropped by 0.3 points on a scale of one to ten, while the 'learning time' was decreased by 2/3rd. However, the students were very satisfied with the multitasking class: they gave it 9.4 out of 10! Two full points higher compared to the evaluation of the normal classes. The students' reactions to the class explained why: 'It wasn't boring,' 'We weren't bored for one second,' and 'We got into some sort of flow.' They did not show any interest in their iPods, messages, the online newspaper, or a snack: the parallel processes of three different flows of data had claimed all of their attention. This had made them feel very energetic and happy (for a moment?).

Social media and the brain

According to Eveline Crone, our brain is fully-grown around the twenty-fifth year of life. She is a professor of developmental psychology at Leiden University in the Netherlands. She is an expert in the field of brain research on teenagers. She uses a technique called Functional Magnetic Resonance Imaging (FMRI) to study the effects of multitasking on the brains of teenagers and adolescents. A teenager's brain seems to react more strongly to positive signals than it reacts to negative signals. This explains why young people are constantly busy searching for stimuli and confirmation and why they are less able to cope with negative criticism and disapproval. This sensitivity to reward-related behavior is produced by the nucleus accumbens (fig 26). This part of the brain is also known as the brain's pleasure center. Whenever any clues that predict possible rewards are present, this produces neural activity in this part of the brain. The nucleus accumbens also plays a part in the ability to assess risks. Sometimes, the prospect of a reward 'beats' the prospect of danger. This may explain why young people sometimes take certain risks, for instance posting erotic pictures on their Facebook page. This imbalance also has its perks. Adolescent brains dispose of the possibility to be creative, idealistic and inventive, according to Crone. The nucleus accumbens is highly susceptible to dopamine, a neuro-transmitter which, as I already mentioned, not only plays an important part in experiencing well-being and pleasure, but also in almost all possible forms of addiction. Excessive dopamine hits can reduce the activity of your brain cells. This leads to a partial blockade of the prefrontal cortex, which causes a person to be less conscious of the implications of their actions. In order for the brain to stay alert, the prefrontal cortex needs to stay active. Manfred Spitzer, Medical Director of the Psychiatric University Hospital of Ulm, Germany, studies dementia. In his book *Digitale Demenz* (2011), he expresses his fear that social media users can develop into some sort of 'reflex' robots. They automatically act in the way in which IT 'demands' them to. According to Spitzer, this could be a cause for the development of early dementia.

The scientists that I mentioned are in fact trying to alert people to the psychological and health-related risks that excessive use of social media could produce.

Are the youngest generations 'dumber' or smarter than the older ones?

Many older people tend to think that children of today are

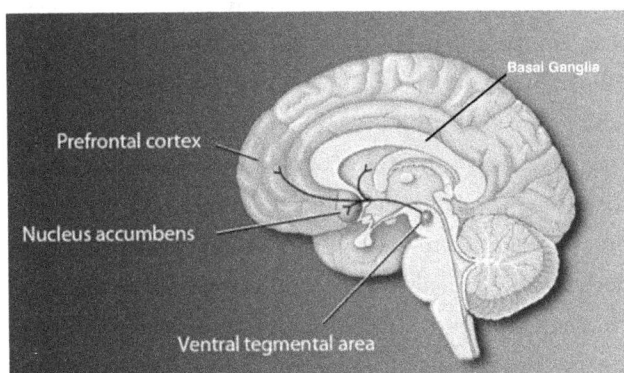

Fig. 25 Nucleus accumbens

less intelligent than they were in their childhood days: 'They are so ignorant.' Children, for their part, consider their grandparents as less intelligent, since 'They do not know how to look anything up on the Internet.' In 2012, Wouter Duyck, Professor of Cognitive Psychology at Ghent University in Belgium, carried out a study on whether or not the Internet makes the juniors of Generation Y dumber people. Young people turned out to be very capable of remembering where to find certain information. They turned out to remember the information they could not look up on the Internet better. The key question remains whether or not this different way of dealing with information makes the members of the youngest generation 'dumber'. Perhaps it shows an evolutionary development, which causes teenagers to be well attuned to the ways of data processing of today and tomorrow?

Dick Swaab, Professor of Neurobiology at the University of Amsterdam, who is known for his studies and publications in the field of brain anatomy and brain physiology, states that our brain size and intelligence has increased enormously in the course of the evolution. By the term 'intelligence', he means the capability to solve problems, the capability to process information, the speed of thinking and the capacity to act in a purposeful way.

Generational differences in the utilization of social media

We studied the differences in utilization of social media on a generational level by carrying out experiments at three different organizations – the Fontys Academy for Creative Industries in Tilburg, the VIAA Reformed College of Higher Education in Zwolle and the district water board of Ridderkerk, the Netherlands. In total, we studied twelve groups, spread over four generations. We asked every peer group what types of social media they used and what skills they were taught by their children or what they had learned from their (grand)parents. We also presented groups of ten-year-olds from the Conscious Generation Z (2000-2015) with the same question at twelve primary schools across the Netherlands. The peer groups answered the questions together. The entire process was recorded by video cameras. A team of researchers analyzed these videos. The following paragraphs summarize the outcomes of our research.

Protest Generation and Connecting Generation X	Pragmatic Generation and Authentic Generation Y
Older generations' tendencies when it comes to the use of social media:	Younger generations' tendencies when it comes to the use of social media:
Discussing the (non)sense of social media	Acting with social media
Searching for instructions and reading these beforehand	Picking up how social media work as they go along
Getting experts to explain devices to them	Posting their questions on LinkedIn or social media to get answers
Exaggerating risks and focused on what could go wrong	Seeing opportunities and trying new things
Drawing up guidelines	Discovering what collectively needs to be agreed upon as they go

Fig. 26 Generations' tendencies when it comes to the use of social media

Seniors from the Protest Generation (1940-1955) are often positively interested in social media. The members of this generation witnessed in their youth many 'firsts', such as the first television broadcast and the first man setting foot on the moon, which might have contributed to a positive curiosity for new things. On the other side, Protest Generation members were very focused on amassing intrinsic knowledge, on retaining gathered information and on obtaining factual knowledge and keeping information in closed systems. They see their (grand)children and younger colleagues using social media to communicate quickly and to share and to look up information. Protest Generation members become acquainted with the possibilities of social media and they follow in young people's footsteps as they gradually start using social media. They start to acknowledge and to experience its advantages step by step. It is estimated that they lag about at least one year behind on their younger colleagues. Some of the Protest Generation members are very interested in social media. They enthusiastically state that a whole new world is opening up for them. According to recent research by Newcom (2017) seniors and elderly are increasingly using YouTube and other social media.

Some Protest Generation members react rather defensively and a small number of seniors assume an embittered attitude towards social media. They wish to hold on to an old-fashioned world that no longer exists and complain about almost everything.

Most of the Protest Generation members think it may cause problems for them if they do not learn how to work with a computer in this modern society. Some older people start using social media later in life, in order to follow and keep in touch with their (grand)children. Most seniors are hesitant about sharing 'everything'. They are shocked by the openness of many teenagers, which they often expose via social media. On the other hand, they experience the openness of juniors from Generation Y as quite disarming. Older people wonder whether these young people are aware of the risks and dangers of social media. However, they themselves are the ones who are not familiar with the actual risks. This can make them feel restless. Their intuition tells them that something can go terribly wrong, but they are unable to point out what exactly can go wrong. This can make them feel paranoid from time to time. This seems to be increased by extremes that are blown up by the media.

The Connecting Generation X (1955-1970) generally assumes a realistic and critical attitude towards the use of social media. When they were young, the first computers were being produced and the precursors to the Internet appeared. Their children were brought up in the digital age. They get to witness the use of social media at very close range. 'When our children come home from school, they immediately go online again to chat with their friends, to whom they have just finished talking at school. It is just nonsense,' some of them said. Partly due to their children's behavior, they are familiar with the different types of social media and they start exploring the possibilities of social media. Xers consider LinkedIn to be the most useful social medium and they use this social network the most. According to them, Facebook is 'full of rubbish.' Half of the Generation Xers have assumed a somewhat skeptical rather than a curious attitude towards the use of social media. Some of the reactions: 'Why would I have to sign up? It takes so much of your time and all you get in return is such nonsense.' 'It seems like you need to "join the club" in order to have a sense of belonging to the rest of the world. I just do not want to be a part of that.' They distinguish their working life from their family life. They set great store by their privacy and they have a hard time understanding the fact that their children post all kinds of 'stuff' on their Facebook page. Xers hardly ever use Twitter, Instagram or Snapchat. They absolutely do not understand why their children choose to use those kinds of media. They do realize that social media can be useful. However, they speak more about the risks than about the possibilities. Perhaps they are worried about the possible negative effects of the use of social media on their children's development.

The Pragmatic Generation (1970-1985) is generally very well informed of the risks and advantages of social media. Pragmatists know very well how to benefit from social media. When they were young, the IT industry emerged. Pragmatists have constructed knowledge e-networks, beyond the bounds of organizations. These e-networks enable us to share knowledge more quickly and more often than ever. From this generation onwards, you are considered smart when you are able to look up relevant information rapidly. Pragmatists are using social media on a daily basis for their jobs. They see the creative possibilities of social media more frequently than the members of older generations. Many Pragmatists wrestle with the question of which type of medium is suited for their private life and which medium is suited for their working life. They use all media in an interchangeable way. A small number of Pragmatic teachers use social media at work as an instrument for feedback. The implementation of social media into their working methods can help them find out what is going on in their class, or to help them ask for the opinion of their students on a class or a test. This gives them the opportunity to act on it. Some of the Pragmatic teachers are of the opinion that it takes too much of their time. Many Pragmatists have integrated the use of social media into everyday life. They use social media whenever they have some time left, for instance on their way to a client or during a lull in a meeting or lecture. The Pragmatic Generation is currently the youngest generation of parents. Pragmatists are quite strict when it comes to their children's use of social media. Pragmatic parents are well aware of the risks of social media. They make sure they alert their children to these risks. Many children who took part in the experiment we carried out in primary schools said that they were not yet allowed to use Facebook and they knew the reasons very well. Their parents restricted the amount of time children were allowed to use the Internet to about 1.5 hours per day.

The juniors from the Authentic Generation Y (1985-2000) form the most enthusiastic generation when it comes to the use of social media. They were brought up with social media and, contrary to other generations, they look up information in real time. Whenever they are having a conversation or when they are attending a meeting and hear something they are not familiar with yet, they look it up on the Internet right away. Or they use the Internet to verify whether a certain statement is correct or not. 'Excuse me, but that point you just made is not completely true, a recent study on the matter has shown the contrary, it says so right here, you see.' They are fervent users of all types of social media, but whether a medium is hot or not can change within a second. They consider LinkedIn as a professional network. It is easy to find kindred spirits and people who are interested in the same things as you are. Y juniors think it is 'kind of funny' that their parents – often Xers – ask them for help. They like to help out their parents. They often think their parents are quite clumsy when it comes to using social media. 'My mom is actually quite clever, but the only thing she can do on the Internet is open her email account and send out an email.' 'My dad has recently signed up for Facebook and now he consistently likes everything I post on my Facebook wall. So annoying.' 'I saw in my Facebook feed that my new nephew had just been born and I told my parents about it the next day. They felt offended because I didn't tell them right away. Why don't they just sign up themselves?'

The newest generation of children, the Conscious Generation Z (2000-2015) considers the Internet and social media as a part of their lives. They pay the same amount of attention to social media as they do to playing outside, playing sports and all other kinds of recreational activities. They do still list playing outside as their most favorite activity. This generation seems to be the conscious users of the Internet and social media. Around their twelfth year of life, they are well aware of the possibilities and they utilize some: they play video games, they do their homework online or they chat with their friends. Social media have been integrated into their everyday lives and this is how they speak of it as well. They are familiar with the terminology and they are aware of the dangers, and they are perfectly well able to indicate specifically what they were taught by their parents, what their parents learned from them and what they are still learning. They seem to find it very normal to try to find a balance between their offline life and their online life. Their parents help them with this by setting clear boundaries for their children. This is something their parents – most of the times Pragmatists – want to do in a non-authoritative way. They say it is better to provide well-founded reasons. This is something that is reflected in research on this generation of children as well. These children are well able to substantiate the reason why they are not allowed to use certain types of social media. Children were able to distinguish between using the Internet for learning purposes and using it for recreational purposes. They are able to reproduce the exact number of hours they spend surfing the Internet per day. This appears to be a quite conscious decision of their parents: social media does not control their lives. They are able to describe how their parents, brothers and sisters use the Internet and social media. They are also aware of the fact that they are more 'media savvy' than their (grand)parents.

Tentative conclusions

Members of the younger generations in the Netherlands are the most familiar with the possibilities of social media and they are the first to figure out how these media can be used in practice. Members of the oldest generations in the Netherlands feel like social media come with certain risks, but they are not able to name them. The older generations dispose of better strategies to search and select. The learning process in applying social media at work seems to be opposite to the process of top-down change and decision making. At home, many (grand)parents learn from their (grand)children how to use social media. At many organizations, the youngest people are predominantly learning from older colleagues instead of (also) the other way around. This one-way learning process is an outdated cultural pattern and is still repeated at many aging organizations that were founded a long time ago, and where a top-down culture is prevalent. Interactive learning is the fresh new pattern, carried on by the youngest generations. Yet, there are other differences that play a part in this as well. Members of older generations tend to focus more on the risks whereas younger generations focus more on opportunities. Members of older generations tend to hit the brakes before people start using social media at work, so they tend to start exploring the possible risks first, preferably with the help of external experts. Members of younger generations, however, wish to encounter and 'tackle' risks as they go along and to put their knowledge, or the knowledge of their peers, to good use. When they need additional expertise, they look it up on the Internet. Despite all these contradictions, seniors from the Protest Generation seem to form the group of people that is best suited to support the youngest generation in introducing the utilization of social media at work. This increases the possibility of a mutual learning development. The juniors will teach seniors how to explore the advantages of social media by working together. The seniors will teach juniors how to develop better search strategies, how to enforce changes within an organization and how to break through outdated patterns within an existing culture. Explorations within various organizations have taught us that members of both generations seem to like the sound of this kind of collaboration.

The youngest working generation is best able to scan what is outdated in how the Internet and social media are used at an organization and best able to see how this can be updated. Seniors are best able to support these juniors in the updating processes, through their knowledge about the culture and their experience with change processes.

10 Social evolution in the Netherlands in the twenty-first century

'Our world upside down'

Our analyses of video recordings of Dutch generations that succeeded each other in different life stages at various Dutch organizations – including 65 videos of groups of Generation Y – produced not only useful information when it comes to generational differences. It also provided insights into the evolution of Dutch social systems, such as organizations, unions and our society. Social patterns that generated the most work energy for new generations of seniors, leaders, mediors, juniors and children, are considered to be the sources of new social trends. The opposite is also true: social patterns that drain away work energy are considered to be patterns that will most likely gradually disappear from society and its institutions. This can be seen as the dying part of a culture. This part is fading out. This can be a process with ups and downs and with a point of no return. A picture like the one painted in fig. 25 can be made more specific for an organization by identifying a top five of energizers and a top five of energy drains for every generation.

The interaction between generations determines the pace of evolutionary development. As the interaction becomes more open and intense, the speed of the social evolution increases. However, every (working) community has its own (natural) pace. If the evolution in a (working) community goes too fast, this will lead to confusion and chaos: the members of the community are not able to process all of the changes. However, if the process goes too slowly, this will be reflected in a decreasing amount of work energy and rising social tensions.

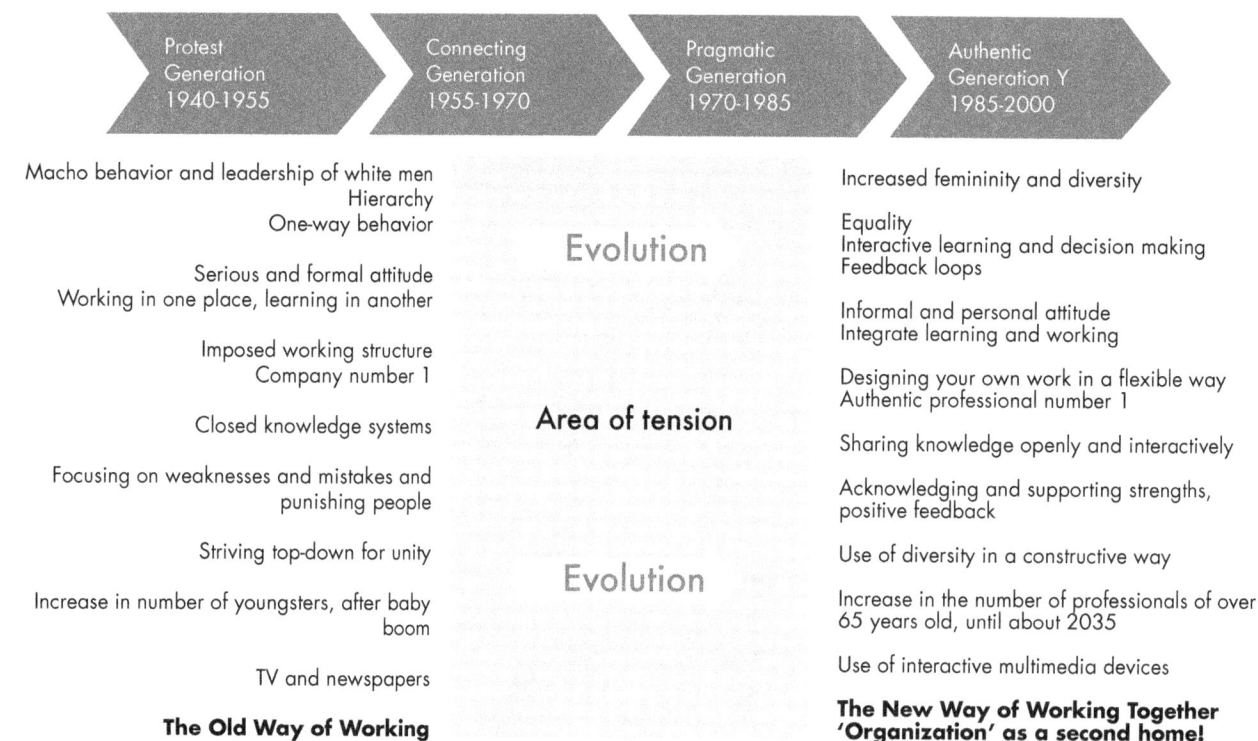

Protest Generation 1940-1955	Connecting Generation 1955-1970	Pragmatic Generation 1970-1985	Authentic Generation Y 1985-2000

Macho behavior and leadership of white men Hierarchy One-way behavior	Evolution	Increased femininity and diversity
Serious and formal attitude Working in one place, learning in another		Equality Interactive learning and decision making Feedback loops
Imposed working structure Company number 1		Informal and personal attitude Integrate learning and working
Closed knowledge systems	Area of tension	Designing your own work in a flexible way Authentic professional number 1
Focusing on weaknesses and mistakes and punishing people		Sharing knowledge openly and interactively
Striving top-down for unity		Acknowledging and supporting strengths, positive feedback
Increase in number of youngsters, after baby boom	Evolution	Use of diversity in a constructive way
TV and newspapers		Increase in the number of professionals of over 65 years old, until about 2035
		Use of interactive multimedia devices
The Old Way of Working		**The New Way of Working Together 'Organization' as a second home!**

Fig. 27 Social-evolutionary trends via successive generations in the Netherlands (and Europe?)

A number of important social trends design the world around us in a way that is new to us. Some of these trends will turn Dutch culture upside down. Or, rather, we ourselves are turning our Dutch world upside down, by permitting and supporting the influence that successive generations have on Dutch (working) society. These are interactive processes, where everybody expresses their feelings and thoughts, with ups and downs and with chaotic periods sometimes. I would like to highlight the most important trends that I see from a generational perspective and to explain them briefly. To conclude, I will mention some possible threats to our social evolution.

Trend 1: Transformation of work and of relationships at work

In this field, seven different effects become visible through subsequent generations. These effects arise simultaneously and they paint a picture of 'the ways of working' in the near future.

1 The distance between managers and employees is getting smaller with every successive generation that I studied. Their relationship is getting more personal. The importance of hierarchy seems to decrease, or even disappear. Hierarchy will not be valued, but whether what you say makes sense.

2 People's need for self-management and equality increases with every new generation and we observe a particularly sharp rise in this from the Pragmatic Generation onwards. It is likely that this is the effect of a transformation in parenting style, in combination with the growing number of people with a high educational level, which increases with every successive generation and will keep on rising at least until Generation Y.

3 From the Pragmatic Generation onwards, working becomes a way of life, which needs to be fun, fulfilling and inspiring. Members of Generation Y have a strong tendency to create their working environment as a 'second home', where they can be authentic and where you have an open,

informal and personal connection with colleagues.

4 From the Pragmatic Generation onwards, work needs to be challenging, needs to be a way to learn and to develop your personality.

5 The process of collaboration is starting to shift towards combining forces for a certain period of time in order to accomplish your mutual goals and to achieve concrete results. The main idea is not to do this within the traditional organizational framework, but to achieve the intended (emotional, ecological and financial) results.

6 Contributing to sustainability is becoming more and more important. The number of companies that are producing and delivering services in a sustainable way is rising. These companies are mentioned by the youngest generation often as most attractive.

7 Internet and social media offer the possibility for knowledge workers to work anywhere they wish.

Trend 2: Open communication, authentic leadership and sharing knowledge

1 From Generation X onwards, communication becomes more and more open, realistic and authentic. More people value different perspectives. This is experienced as a richer way of looking that generates deeper knowledge about things and stimulates innovation. From the Pragmatic Generation onwards, people's attitude has become more open. Mutual interaction is becoming faster and more intense. Thanks to the advent of social media. The popularity of social media has led to a boom in the sharing of opinions and findings. From Generation Y onwards, communication as a whole becomes more spontaneous, personal and direct. These youngsters communicate faster, more often and on a more international scale with each other than any former generation has ever done.

2 The power of people is shifting from 'a focus on the authorities' (Silent Generation) via democratic decision making

and a focus on majorities for an idea (Protest Generation) to the increasingly independent professionalism of the Pragmatic Generation and the Authentic Generation Y professionals, towards a focus on the professional as a person. And then to a triple focus: planet, people and sustainable evolution.

3 Dutch leadership shifts from 'male dominance and convincing others of your own ideals' (Protest Generation), via becoming more realistic and conscious together, connecting diversity and a coaching style (Generation X), towards paying explicit attention to professional development (Pragmatic Generation) and supporting the authentic development of professionals at work (Generation Y).

4 The meaning of knowledge and the way people deal with knowledge is changing as well. The members of the Protest Generation used to lock up their knowledge in closed systems. Having knowledge was power. Generation X encouraged the utilization of different perspectives and fields of knowledge when it comes to solving difficult issues. The Pragmatic Generation constructed (and is still constructing) open knowledge networks, across organizational boundaries as a way to share and provide knowledge quickly in order to solve problems in a practical way. Generation Y has become very skilled in the art of looking up information and making optimum use of social media. The members of the youngest generation of children (Generation Z) handle knowledge in a remarkably open way and they are even more social-media savvy.

5 Increasing use of social media stimulates knowledge sharing, across boundaries between organizations, industries and countries.

Trend 3: Vitality, sustainability in human energy and late retirement

Over the past 50 years, average life expectancy has increased by 7.9 years. Average male life expectancy has increased to 79.2 in the Netherlands (Statistics Netherlands, 2011). For Dutch women, it increased to 82.9 years. In Southern European countries, life expectancy is even higher.

The members of the current generation of seniors are more vital around their sixtieth year of life than their predecessors were at that age. The working population of over-60s has increased from 12 percent in 2001 to 43 percent in 2010. Many people over sixty years old wish to stay vital for a long time. The motto of 'working keeps you vital' seems to become a trend. The retirement age will have been upped to rise to 66 by 2020, and 67 by 2025.

Increasing state spending alone will force governments to focus policy on stimulating people to continue working after they have reached the current retirement age. Without such a focus on extending people's working lives, the ratio of active citizens to non-active citizens will be two to one by 2040. This ratio was seven to one in 1957 and it was four to one in 2010. Aside from this, slightly increasing economic activity means that companies will have to attract seniors in order to get all of the work done. Seniors form the only population group in the Netherlands that is able to realize a rise in labor participation.

The members of the youngest generation are aware of the fact that they are likely to have to continue working into old age, possibly until or after the age of seventy. This will encourage them to manage their work energy carefully. Many of them are searching for ways that will increase their energy at work, in order to make their human 'battery' last longer. The fact that their aim is to find 'a fun job that matches their personality' is in keeping with this development. The word 'fun' might sound a bit superficial, but when you ask what they mean by this word, a deeper layer comes forward: an open-minded and informal culture, spontaneous feedback from colleagues, freedom to innovate. The juniors have learned from the non-vital seniors what the don'ts in working life are: 'Do not allow yourself to be forced into a direction that does not suit your energy. It will destroy your growth and development as a human being and as a professional worker and it will shorten your (working) life and, last but not least, it will make you unhappy and unfulfilled.'

Trend 4: The feminization of (Dutch) organizations

The values that all generations we studied shared indicated that a rather feminine culture is taking hold at Dutch organizations. In every next generation, we found that more women had more impact on men. The highest-scoring values are: living a healthy life, being honest, being competent and having self-respect, self-confidence and respect for others. The lowest-scoring values are: being immortal, playing the hero, acting like a tough guy and having power. It is most likely that this feminization will continue. Every Dutch successive generation that I studied starts to show more feminine behavior. This is a result of the increased number of working women in connection with the increased mutual interaction and equality between men and women, and a strong increase in the educational level of women. From the Pragmatic Generation onwards, the number of leading women has been rising strongly. The results of my recent study regarding the characteristics of the newest generation of children, the Conscious Generation Z (2000-2015), indicate that – I would like to put this as delicately as possible, because it might need more research – the leadership of girls in the youngest Dutch generation is developing early. Dutch girls develop their sense of leadership more energetically and with more ease than boys do. An international literature review and our analyses of video recordings of Dutch generations have shown that women are more focused on connecting and making personal contact with others, more on expressing and sharing their emotions, listening and on working together than men. Increasing man/woman integration in the Netherlands, and thus the increasing influence of women on men, results in

the fact that younger generations start to show more appreciation for learning processes, collaboration, openness and personal relationships. I expect that around 2023 about 50 % of the Dutch leaders will be women and around 2030 about 70 %. Perhaps, at the same time a countermovement will arise: a revaluation of male qualities, coexisting harmoniously with the female qualities.

This trend also means that boys who are raised in a macho non-Dutch culture or in families where macho behavior is stimulated have difficulties in being accepted. Their macho behavior will meet with negative reactions.

Trend 5: The way towards continual development and evolutionary change

Successive generations have changed the nature of change processes from 'democratic decision making, employing top-down idealistic change management and a focus on restructuring' (Protest Generation), to coaching and doing what have been proved to be successful processes – evidence-based change – (Generation X), to improving the situation at hand step by step in a practical way (Pragmatic Generation), to a continuing process of realizing small, direct changes and real-time feedback (Generation Y), executed by professionals themselves, facilitated by their managers. In short: change processes will turn into continual updating processes in everyday working life, supported by 'managers'. I expect that the phenomenon of evolutionary change will become a trend: it will become a way of constant renewal from within the professional heart of the organization, with a strong focus on changes that generate work energy and vitality. At many bigger organizations, all generations consider top-down control management and change the number one cause of decreasing work energy and increasing tensions. Tension particularly starts to mount at organizations that employ many professionals with a high level of education. Tension arises when colleagues and managers from older generations hold on to certain outdated habits for too long – generally not because they want to act in this way but because they are trapped in these routines. Such outdated patterns conflict with the fresh new cultural patterns that are being developed by younger generations.

Trend 6: Growing attention for diversity and integration

With every new generation, our society becomes more and more diverse. Or stated in another way, our society and its institutions and organizations are diverse and all those diverse groups want to be equally respected and want to co-create the community in which they are participating. This is also reflected in the number of political parties that entered Dutch parliamentary elections in 2017. There have never been as many parties, twenty-eight, and there was not one dominating party. The need to learn to cooperate in groups and teams with 'minorities' is growing.

More frequent stimulating diversity in teams is considered to be a strategy that can be used in order to activate innovation, creativity and flexibility in organizations.

In the course of this process of growing diversity, the following four developments are observed:

1 The number of working women in the Netherlands has increased strongly over the past decades. The percentage was 52 percent in 1997, and from 2008 onwards, it has stabilized around 61 percent, according to data provided by Statistics Netherlands. The educational level of women is increasing. From the Pragmatic Generation onwards, more women (43%) than men (35%) have a higher educational level. During the past two decades, the number of female PhD students has doubled to five in ten

2 The percentage of working migrants in the Netherlands, the ethnic diversity, increases with every successive generation, and from Generation Y onwards, we expect to observe a sharp rise in this development

In 2017, the Dutch population reached 17.1 million. In 2035, we expect to have 18 million inhabitants. Population growth will largely come on the back of immigration, as the rate of immigration is higher than the birth rate. Expectations are that about 185,000 immigrants will be added to the population every year until about 2035.

The educational level of young migrants is increasing, in particular the educational level of young female migrants. Between 1996 and 2010, the number of non-Western immigrants in university education has tripled. The number of foreign students in the Netherlands increased from 8.1 to 8.4 percent in 2012. For the first time, more than 10,000 foreign students were studying in the Netherlands. The number of Dutch students studying abroad has risen to 46,300. Young asylum seekers are doing well at school, 39 % are on their way to higher education. Free movement of people across the European Union makes it easier for European migrants to move to other European countries. An increasing number of small to medium-sized enterprises are internationally active. International mobility is growing.

According to data provided by the Dutch Social and Economic Council, the number of economic migrants in the Netherlands has tripled to 350,000 since 2004. Almost 80 percent of these migrants are from EU member states. Amsterdam has a population of 800,000, originating from 180 different countries. Almost seventeen percent of all Dutch employees work for companies that are controlled from abroad. These companies represent 32 percent of the Netherlands' gross domestic product. The recent (2016) wave of refugees from Syria, who seem to be better educated and who seem to be more driven to participate in our society, might contribute towards more diversity in society and institutions. But we do not know what effects EU and Dutch government measures aimed at reducing and controlling this stream of immigrants will have. And we do not know the results of the interaction between proponents and opponents of immigration in our society. These outcomes can change the attitude towards immigrants in a way that makes our country less attractive for them to live and work in. However, I expect the attitude towards immigrants to ultimately be positive.

In 2016, I asked in three multicultural groups what they preferred, a team with colleagues from their own country or a team with people from different countries. They said that they, with no doubt, preferred a very multicultural team, with no dominance of any ethnic group. The main reason was that they learned much from each other's perspectives and that it keeps them awake.

Types of diversity	A member of the Protest Generation	A member of Generation X	A member of Pragmatic Generation	A member of Generation Y
'Hierarchic' levels	Reduces distance between employer and employee	Reduces distance, leaders stand more next to the people, instead of feeling superior	Reduces distance, strives for diversity and discusses the theme pragmatically	Assumes an equal attitude, is used to equality at home
Gender	Talks about reducing distance, but does not really act on it	Reduces distance, strives for diversity but there still exists some tension between men and women	Assumes an equal attitude, already at school	Assumes an equal attitude
Functional	Creates distance via parochialism	Reduces distance by working in multifunctional teams	Reduces distance by combining different sources of knowledge	Assumes an equal attitude, pays attention to making a valuable contribution
Ethnic		Makes the issue discussible	Reduces distance, is open-minded when it comes to diversity	Assumes an equal attitude. Has become acquainted with the theme of diversity at school. Growth of international mobility
Age		Assumes an equal attitude towards youngest generation at home, maintains distance towards oldest generation and to the youngest at work	Reduces distance, strives for equality. However, there is still some tension between them and members of the Protest Generation	Assumes an equal attitude, does not experience any distance; does not react based on age but based on vitality of seniors
Educational level			Emancipation of smart go-getters with lower educational level arises	Emancipation of smart go-getters with lower educational level breaks through

Fig. 28 Every generation's contribution to the integration of diversity in society

1   The number of specializations within different fields is increasing as a consequence of a professionalization surge that has been going on over the past decades and as a consequence of the increased number of disciplines. More and more frequently, experts work together, using terms such as 'chain integration' or 'program management', and surpassing the boundaries of organizations, in order to solve complicated matters.

The increasing automation and robotization of routine work might stimulate this process and might stimulate the development of human skills that cannot be copied by computers.

2   Age diversity in the Dutch workforce will rise over the coming decades. Seniors will continue working longer than before and juniors wish to combine both learning and working. At the same time, an emancipatory process seems to be taking place for both seniors and juniors. Many seniors from the Protest Generation wish to contribute actively for as long as possible. Juniors from Generation Y wish to contribute as soon as they start working. Generation X has put the theme of diversity on the map. The new leaders from Generation X are searching for ways to connect and exploit this increasing diversity. Generation Y is the most skilled generation when it comes to handling all types of diversity. Many members of the youngest working generation have become acquainted with the ethnic diversity of today at school, as they were growing up. Many students choose to do a work placement abroad and/or travel around the world for a few months, either alone or with their friends. The act of experiencing different ethnicities forms a new element for this new rising generation of juniors. A study that I carried out in collaboration with the Timing employment agency regarding the difference in educational level between different members of the same generation showed that an emancipatory process of professionals with a lower educational level sets in from the Pragmatic Generation onwards, they want more attention and more respect as smart doers.

Aside from this, every new generation becomes more skilled in handling the growing diversity in our working community. This does not mean that this trend will be just as powerful in every industry or organization. There are trendsetters and trend followers.

Trend 7: Increasing IQ (?), EQ and SQ

Up until now, the average IQ of every successive generation has increased by ten points. This was shown in a study carried out by James Flynn. He stated that in the Netherlands, this development could be the consequence of a combination of factors, such as a healthier diet, a rise of the number of people with a higher educational level, and, in comparison to other countries, more intensive interaction among contemporaries. According to neurobiologist Dick Swaab (2010), the size of our brain and our intelligence – the capability to process information and to solve problems – has increased tremendously from generation to generation. However, the Netherlands Institute for Social Research has found that recently an increasing number of autochthonous sons have a lower level of education than their autochthonous fathers. For more information, please refer to the paragraph entitled 'Possible threats to our social evolution,' at the end of this chapter. This trend brings forward the question of what this might mean for Dutch society, will future generations be less smart than their predecessors? The Emotional Quotient (EQ) indicates to what extent a person will be successful or able to find their way in (working) life (Goleman, 1995). The extent to which someone is able to handle their emotions in a constructive way and to recognize and acknowledge someone else's emotions can be of importance. Analyses of our video recordings have shown that members of the Pragmatic Generation tend to hold back their emotional expressions, but that they do rationally speak about them with a little more ease. It appears that members of Generation Y are most in touch with their emotions. The Conscious Generation Z seems to take this sensitivity to the next level. Zers are very spontaneous and expressive people.

The increasing feminization of every new working generation ensures that the social skill (the social quotient, SQ) to work together improves in varying contexts. At many Dutch primary schools, children work/learn in teams of about five children, every day. At some schools, older children support the youngest ones. Every next generation that I studied is more focused on collaboration (at a young age), which is highly likely to lead to a higher SQ.

Possible threats to our social evolution

Obesity

In the Netherlands, the phenomenon of obesity is starting to become an important social problem. No less than 55 percent of men and 50 percent of the women are overweight. According to Statistics Netherlands (2011), the number of young people who suffer from moderate obesity has increased from seven to eleven percent. Out of these people, 2.5 percent suffer from severe obesity. Moderate obesity has increased from 28 to 36 percent for adults. Severe obesity has increased from five percent around 1985 to twelve percent in 2011. Up until now, we have been more interested in the health risks of severe obesity, in the psychological and social problems and in the declining quality of life. There are not many articles on the effects of obesity on our IQ, SQ and EQ, the effects on how we function. It definitely makes people unable to work and affects the quality of working life.

Stagnation in the increase of the Dutch educational level

Stagnation in the increasing educational level is already visible for autochthonous men. In their report called *'Generatiewisseling'*, the Netherlands Institute for Social Research uses the terms 'upward' and 'downward educational mobility'. The sharp rise in the number of people with a higher educational level in the second half of the previous century implied that a high percentage of sons had a higher educational level than their fathers. The same goes for daughters and mothers. The Netherlands Institute for Social Research observed that there is a risk of a decline in the upward educational mobility for autochthonous sons. This turning point has not been observed for autochthonous daughters, neither for the sons and daughters of immigrants. In the coming decades, autochthonous sons might have a lower educational level than their fathers. This causes an increasing chance of the rise of the average educational level stagnating. This creates an image of a young generation that has a lower educational level than previous generations. And the question that will be asked is whether we have reached the limit of what the current educational system is able to contribute to the further development of our (working) intelligence. A growing percentage of Dutch children are more stressed about their studies. This can be considered as an early warning sign, namely of the risk that putting top-down pressure on these children in order to improve academic records will work out all wrong. This development also alerts us to the risk of a decline in teachers' work energy, in students' learning energy and in academic performance. This top-down pressure pattern has passed its expiration date. Life-long learning offers opportunities for the time being, but how long will it continue to do so? We need innovations in the educational system in order to find new learning methods. Making use of the head start that children have compared to their teachers when it comes to using social media seems such an obvious new method.

High-quality education and excellent academic performance are generally considered as predictors of a favorable socio-economic development in a country. It is safe to say that it is of great importance to us all to invent new educational methods.

Outdating in cultures

The phenomenon of population aging will increase until the year 2035. As I mentioned before: if aging results in the fact that outdated methods of older generations keep dominating new patterns introduced by younger generations, the culture in question will become outdated (at organizations: the collective working intelligence). In all probability, this will have negative consequences for the quality of our products and services. One of the most important challenges for the coming decades seems to be to figure out how we will be able to exploit the increasing amount of expertise and (working) wisdom of the expanding group of seniors. We need to find out how the collaboration between fresh juniors and experienced seniors can lead to a new way of applying existing knowledge, and we need to find out how to optimally support the refreshing influence of young generations, of which the number of members keeps decreasing with every subsequent youngest generation.

Up until today, Dutch students are not prepared to deal with the risks and advantages of the many gradually aging companies. They are thrown, so to say, in at the deep end when it comes to steering clear of the energy-draining outdated patterns of their older colleagues. They did not learn how to profit from the growing availability of experience at aging companies.

11 A summary of essentials, three matters of discussion and suggestions for future generation research

A summary of essentials

In this book, I have shared with the reader the results of 20 years of generational research and of supporting new generations in the Netherlands in updating their organizations (or better: organizational culture). One of the most important findings during my research is that culture patterns, such as ways of leading, cooperating, communicating, organizing, learning, acting with diversity and so on, have an expiration date. Like food has. After this date, these patterns become energy drains for the people that repeat them and become life threatening for a company or institution. Successive generations in a life phase play a key role in refreshing these outdated culture patterns. This process of organizational (culture) evolution is currently stagnating at many aging Dutch companies. Interventions can reignite the evolutionary development.

At aging organizations, the oldest generations are the largest. Members of older Dutch generations have a natural tendency to repeat outdated culture patterns blindly, to repeat automatically what they have been used to doing for so many years. Even when doing so means allowing their energy to be drained away. As soon as the group of seniors becomes aware of this effect, the process of updating can start. Members of the youngest generation can scan the outdated patterns quickly and clearly. This can speed up this process of raising awareness. The power of the youngest generation to scan outdated patterns is often underestimated.

At aging organizations, the youngest generations are the smallest. They have the natural tendency to update outdated culture patterns. They are most sensitive to outdated parts of the culture of their working community and experience emotional, physical and mental resistance to repeating them. When they are forced to repeat them or when they adapt, the loss of energy can be seen in real organizational life and on video within a couple of minutes. Repeating

outdated patterns is like going down a dead end road. The energy loss will decrease the survival power of that company. The company will become less attractive to (young) employees and clients. In the worst-case scenario, it may mean the end of the company.

Many Dutch companies have a strong focus on the youngest generation at work. Often, expectations of their fresh impact on the culture are high. This can be a trap and lead to disappointment. The power of this smallest generation at work to implement change is often overestimated. They need the openness and support of the larger older generations. For many aging organizations and institutions in the Netherlands and in many other European countries, their economic, social and ecological future depends on whether they can generate the youthfulness of all generations at work, from the youngest to the oldest. This youthfulness, which is the evolutionary power of a generation to keep their own culture up to date, can be found in the top five of their most important energizers. Each generation comes up with a different top five, reflecting the fact that they have been raised differently. It also means that the evolutionary focus of each generation is on refreshing another part of their culture.

The most difficult moment in these evolutionary processes is when fresh culture patterns come up against the wall of existing culture, when fresh culture patterns are confronted with outdated patterns. When what you do is different from what everybody at your company has been used to doing for so many years. When you are a vital 65-year-old senior from the Protest Generation – the new generation of seniors – and you say: 'I do not want to leave the company at all. I want flexible hours, I love to work together with the youngest professionals and learn new things. I at least want to be able to choose when I retire. I understand that the value of my expertise is important in this.' This does not tally with the outdated thoughts many managers have of elderly people. Or, when you are a junior from the Authentic Generation Y and you respond to your manager who asks you to put your fresh new idea on paper: 'I do not want to put my idea on paper and for you to discuss it with your management team. I want you to support me in getting seven colleagues together who are the best in this field and I want to ask them to join me in this thought process, and I want to use Prezi to present my idea.' Colleagues around this person might react in a way that could be interpreted as a sign that you have to go back to the old routine. Sometimes they even say so explicitly: 'Let us do it in the way we always have.' Maybe you do not believe me, but I have checked it many times; unwillingly adapting to outdated routines of (older) generations is not appreciated at all by these seniors. So, keep that in mind and always check your interpretation. For instance, by saying: 'Do you really want me to adapt unwillingly to that outdated routine, which is draining my energy away? And what about you? I see that the same is happening to you, but you seem not to be aware of it.' Renewing outdated culture patterns can be exciting. You will almost never get prior permission to renew a deep-rooted outdated pattern. The most important moment is when you dare to do it. After a certain period of time, others start to repeat the new pattern(s) that you introduced. It will really break through when they start to experience the benefits, when they experience the energy boost. It is an adventure because you are looking across the boundaries of your culture, into the unknown world, for updates that will strengthen the survival power of your team and your company. A golden rule for updaters who want to increase these evolutionary processes of renewing outdated culture patterns, is the following:

Stay connected, both to yourself and to your (senior) colleagues around you, even when they show uneasiness and resistance. Ask questions and share your feelings about the situation. Stay free and connected at the same time. For instance, by asking them in a personal way what they want from you and listening carefully to their answer. Tell them what you want, learn from what they say and do what your positive energy 'tells' you to do. Respect your professional friends and do also what your instinct – reflected in rising energy levels – tells you to do.

Juniors need support and feedback of seniors to find their own way. The juniors could organize support themselves. Seniors can offer their support as soon as they see the energy loss in a junior. Do not hold back as a senior when you see youngsters acting in a way that generates resistance or uneasiness in you. Being open-minded towards the working methods and feedback of young people stimulates healthy interaction. An open mind and open attitude makes it more likely that young people will want to cooperate with you. These effects often boost your work energy levels and make work more fun.

If you, as a senior, feel like you are adapting unwillingly to the behavior of the younger generation, you might be on the wrong path. Check your energy levels. When these are down, this might be a sign that, evolutionarily speaking, you are on the wrong path. Share this experience. Once you have shared with them how you feel, healthy interaction and collaboration can be re-established, which will create mutual energy at work.

Sometimes, it might be hard for a senior to collaborate with young people. For instance, when you start to doubt something and you are convinced of the fact that this is not the right way to go, because your experience tells you otherwise. Not saying anything and giving the members of the younger generation the benefit of the doubt turns out all wrong. It is a better idea to share your doubts, without imposing them, and to have an open mind as to whether they are wrong or right. Articulate your doubts clearly and start searching for solutions together and stay on an equal footing. If you are open to the idea that the oldest and the youngest generations can learn the most from each other, this is a fresh attitude that will stimulate juniors to open up to senior experience. Most members of the new generation of juniors of today – Generation Y – will not be open to learning from the experiences of seniors as long as seniors are not open to learning from Yers as well. The fresh new pattern is to learn from each other in a mutual and interactive way.

Leaving behind the patterns that are 'deeply embedded in our brain', as Victor Lamme states, can be accompanied by strong feelings. At first, feelings of denial, sadness and confusion might rise. When you are open to those emotions, this inner process can turn to clearness and turn to awareness of what is going on. This is when you become aware of how you automatically repeat a deep-rooted outdated routine, which is also depleting your energy levels. Step by step, you will find a way to renew it.

Matters of discussion

The most discussed matters during my 'generation master classes and workshops' in the Netherlands are: 1) Does each generation really span a period of fifteen years? 2) Are generational differences caused by age, by the zeitgeist or by the generation itself? 3) Is one generation better than the other?

Fifteen-year cycle
In the last two centuries, several well-known European philosophers, social and historical scientists mentioned this cycle (see fig. 6). However, their theory is based on deep thinking about generations, not on what we today consider to be good scientific research. Two directions of ideas can be distinguished: a) the biological rhythm of birth and death has an impact on the generational cycle, b) a generation is

'born' in a certain age, which is defined by historical events, such as wars or deep economical crises. I found a third one that might be closer to reality.

I think that the rhythm of generations is based on the natural interaction between parents and children. This interaction is most intense during the first life phase (0-15). At the end of this phase, in puberty, children make a transition from childhood to (the beginning) of adulthood. Can I prove that this interaction shapes the basis of a generation and the basis of the rhythm of 15 years? Not yet. But many sessions with Dutch generations of juniors and Dutch generations of children and with the generations of their parents have led me to this insight.

Between 2000 and 2007, I looked around in the (scientific) world for books and articles about generations, but I did not find any book or article with a division of generations that was based on 'good' scientific research. In 2013, a Dutch student (Candel, 2013) collected articles and books about the American Millennials (1985-2000). He did not find a clear generation theory underpinning the American generational division.

However, the question why new generations were 'born' in 1940, 1955, 1970, 1985, 2000 and 2015 and so on is not answered. Two large-scale research projects in the Netherlands showed that the division that is used in this book is the right one, at least in the Netherlands and probably in the so-called Western world, in countries with cultural characteristics that are similar to those in the Netherlands. About 80 % of the Dutch participants recognized this division and the characteristics of the generations. Even though we do not know why generations are divided by a 15-year time span, you can take it as a given and make a generational division on this assumption. This division can be checked. When about 80 % of the participants recognize the division, it must be the right one. I mentioned already that about 20 % of the people do not feel a connection to their own generation.

Scientific generation research

I have found that questionnaires and even deep interviews fail to unearth what generations do and how they differ. Firstly, what people think that they (will) do is not similar to what they really do. Victor Lamme (2010) showed that MRI scans are better predictors of people's behavior than questionnaires. Secondly, most people have limited awareness of their daily behavior. Thirdly, when you want to know what the preferences or energizers are of a generation, you have to ask a group from that generation. A better way is to see how they behave. Individual behavior is not the same as generation behavior. Gottman showed that analyzing videotapes of the behavior of couples was an efficient scientific methodology to get an insight into their interactions. I used this methodology in my generation research. See the appendix for the research methodology that I developed.

Are generational differences caused by age, zeitgeist or by the generation itself?
To unravel this scientific knot, you have to look at generations from an evolutionary perspective. This perspective is based on the generation theory that I developed.

First, as I wrote before, the most important characteristics of a newborn generation are created through the interaction between parents and children in the first phase of children's lives (0-15 years). These characteristics are created by changes in the way parents raise their children, compared to how they were raised by their parents. Most Dutch parents

from the same generation have about the same way of raising their children. They do not change everything in their parenting style. The way Connecting Generation X raised their Authentic Generation Y children is a mix of new ways and a repetition of what they experienced in their childhood as good ways of raising children. What has changed and is becoming typical of the generation of their children are the sources of fresh new culture patterns for the surrounding culture(s). The generation of their children brings these fresh new patterns into the existing world around them, which was built by former generations. The older generations are the carriers of the existing culture. During the second life phase (15-30 years) the younger generation enters institutions and organizations and becomes an active participant in society. When the older generations open themselves up to the fresh new patterns of the youngest generation, this will trigger a process of integration of fresh new patterns into the existing culture. When the older generations do not open themselves up to these new culture patterns, tensions between the older and the youngest generation will rise. Right up to the phase of leadership, a generation's power to change things will keep growing.

Do historical events have an impact on the characteristics of a generation? In their first life stage, historical events might have impact on the way they are raised by their parents. What also seems important to me is how a generation itself reacts to historical events. For instance, the Dutch Authentic Generation Y reacted relaxed and optimistic during the economic crisis between 2007 and 2014, which happened to be the period when they entered the labor market. Along the way, they worried about getting a job, but in the meantime, they accepted jobs without a contract or with a low salary. Some of them opted to stay in education, some took a year off and travelled the world.

Do technical innovations have an impact on a generation? Yes and no. The world is changing all the time. Generations develop within that changing world. We have noticed in our research into generational differences with respect to the use of social media that the youngest generations learn faster how to use the newest social media and have a stronger tendency to experiment. The older generations follow the younger ones, with a delay of about a year. Technical innovations have an impact on all generations, they change the way people interact with each other, how they learn, how they get information and so on.

Is one generation better than another?

My viewpoint is that every generation is equally good (and bad). Every generation has its strengths and weaknesses. My research was focused on the evolutionary value of a generation and not on their weaknesses. A historical study of generations might lead to differences in their contribution to the evolution of their society and its institutions. However, their contribution depends also on the openness and support of the older generations. An historical overview might show how they played their evolutionary role. In the 1990s, the Dutch Connecting Generation X was called the lost generation. However, twenty years later research showed that they were not lost at all. In the 1990s, the Protest Generation was seen as the generation that built the so-called polder model and contributed to the economic boom after WWII. However, in the first decade of this century, leaders from this generation were seen as causers of the economic and environmental crises. This might be true. From my perspective, crises are caused by the repetition of outdated culture patterns. However, such repetition is the result of the interaction between older and younger generations. All existing generations are involved. Open and intense interaction speeds up replacement of outdated patterns by new ones. Closed and weak interaction does the exact opposite.

Ideas for future generation research

Generation research in Brazil, Belgium and in three European young professional networks has shown that the characteristics of the youngest generations were about the same. The interaction between generations was quite different. Future generation research in cultures that differ strongly from each other might teach us more about this issue.

In 2017, my research in the Netherlands will be about the best way to support the small young generation in updating their surrounding aging culture at work. In parallel, I will try to find out what can be done to stimulate their parents, who are generally from the Connecting Generation X (1955-1970), to cooperate at work with these young professionals in the same way as they do successfully at home. You could look at this issue this way: when there is a disconnect between the generation in the leadership phase and the youngest generation of professionals, this is most likely due to the fact that many parents interact with their children's contemporaries at work in a way that differs significantly from how they interact with that same generation (their children) at home.

In 2018, new generation-related issues will arise in the Netherlands, such as how to prepare the next youngest and even smaller generation, born between 2000 and 2015, for work life at spectacularly aging organizations. The first cohorts of this generation will enter work life within a couple of years.

Appendix 1
Towards a scientific method for generational research

Introduction

The first organization to take part in my doctoral research around 2002 was the Dutch fire department. After I had done sixty in-depth interviews with the most energetic managers of the fire department from three different generations, I was able to conclude that interviews and questionnaires were not useful for generational research. The participants could not describe the characteristics of their own and of the other generations, but many of them had the feeling that there were at least some differences. During the interviews, I started to ask members of the Protest Generation to describe the characteristics of their own children (of the Pragmatic Generation): 'In what way do your children differ from you?' The answers varied from, 'No idea, I have actually never thought of that' to 'Well, I certainly have the feeling that there are differences between their generation and mine, but I am having a hard time pointing them out.' One of them said, 'I think that they are faster in a way.' Interviews with managers at different other organizations showed the same results.

This led me to some important conclusions:
1) Feeling that there are some differences could mean that the differences are there 'under your nose', every day, you sense it, but you cannot put your finger on them.
2) Interviews and questionnaires are of no help when it comes to generation-characterizing behavior of which we are not aware.
3) I had to find a research methodology that could support the participants and researchers to become aware of social patterns characterizing a generation..

I also asked these managers (a) to describe their most successful projects and (b) to explain which of their actions made their projects successful. Text analyses of the parts with their actions brought forward some differences be-

tween generations (Bontekoning, 2007). However, this was a very time consuming way to find generational differences in behavior.

While I was puzzling over the question of which scientific method would be more effective and best suit my research, three important things happened.

First of all, I discovered that members of the Pragmatic Generation were in fact able to indicate certain characteristics of the Protest Generation during a group interview, when they tried to do so *together*. This often started hesitantly with someone saying something like, 'They do debate an awful lot,' followed by someone else saying, 'Yes, now that you put it like that, I totally recognize that!' Every interviewee came up with a small part of the entirety of characterizing features of the Protest Generation. The other interviewees recognized some of the characteristics after somebody else had mentioned it; having someone else pointing it out for them made them become aware of these features. This enabled them to paint a picture of the characteristic social patterns of the Protest Generation. This means that group members can help each other in becoming more conscious of social patterns. Of course, there is always the risk of socially desirable behavior interfering with the research. By videotaping these sessions, I was able to pick up on this kind of behavior. You can even score the participants' answers on their level of reliability.

Second of all, I noticed that the Pragmatic Generation displayed generation-characterizing behavior as they were working together with their peers on finding group answers to some questions: they cooperated and communicated in a way that is typical of their generation. At the same time, I became aware of the simple fact that, if I want generational answers to some questions, I have to ask a generation; a group of seven to nine seemed to be sufficient to get generational answers.

Thirdly, I read the book *Blink* by Malcolm Gladwell to find out more about the phenomenon of subconsciously processing information. Gladwell describes a study on married couples, carried out by John Gottman, a psychologist at the University of Washington. By means of video analysis of interactions of married couples, Gottman was able to predict with 95% certainty whether or not these couples would still be together fifteen years later. He discovered that even the analysis of 'thin slices', video parts consisting of a few minutes out of a video of an hour, yielded very accurate predictions, especially when he focused on emotion patterns. Even better predictions were achieved by watching the same 'thin slices' twice and by focusing on a selection of the behavior. Gottman asked married couples to talk about a subject that they deemed important. Every married couple appeared to create certain patterns, which were typical of their own particular way of communicating, of which they were not aware. This told me that analyzing video recordings of generations carrying out a group task enables a small group of researchers to become aware of and analyze social patterns that are typical of that particular generation. By a group task, I mean a real one, not something fake. The task must be real and important for the generation group. For instance, this is the case when the group really believes that they contribute to research that could bring forward new ways of keeping their company up to date and vital. Interaction within the research team also raised awareness of certain social patterns.

Later in my research, I discovered that by asking a generation group to make a top five together of their energizers at work, I was able to gain insight into their most important social patterns. These patterns also came forward in the top five and how they made the top five.

Generation research methodology

These discoveries are the ingredients for an efficient and effective method to help forge scientific study of behavioral characteristics of generations. This method works as follows:

1 A small group of people (seven to nine), consisting of the most energetic members of the same generation (in an organization) is assembled. The most energetic members form the vanguard and display the strongest generational characteristics.

2 This generational group works on a 'real task' for about an hour. The task is given to the generation group on paper. They execute their task in their own specific way of communicating, collaborating, leading, etc., which is typical of their particular generation. The task is to draw up a top five of 'energizers' and a top five of 'energy drains'. The answers provide important information about what their cultural updates are and what is outdated in their surrounding culture.

3 The whole process is videoed.

4 The video recordings are analyzed by a (small) research team that focuses on generation-characterizing social patterns and levels of emotion and energy. A larger research team stimulates a more objective analysis.

5 The fragments containing the most generation-characterizing patterns and their top five of energizers are selected and put together on a tape.

6 This summary is presented to the generational group concerned, so the group can verify the summary's accuracy.

This method is a combination of a group interview and a video analysis of the group behavior (of the generation as a subculture). The group interview yields collective answers to relevant questions. The video recordings offer the possibility to select and paint a picture of the most important behavioral characteristics of a generation.

Repeatability and verifiability
Different research teams can analyze the same video summaries. The research procedure lends itself for repetition of the experiment, both with the same generational group as with a group from the same generation in different organizations.

Independence, objectivity/intersubjectivity
One or more small teams of researchers can carry out analysis of the video recordings. As the number of researchers/team of researchers increases, the intersubjectivity increases. The participants can also test the video summary for accuracy.

Testability and reliability
Reliability can be tested in different ways, such as by making sure the room, the organization, the size of the group, the questions and the procedure are exactly the same for each generation that takes part in the experiment. Reliability can also be tested by studying the same generation at different companies, by asking different research teams to analyze the same video summary of typical behavioral patterns, or by asking the same research team to analyze the same video summary several times.

Validity and generalization
Validity and generalization increase as characterizing behavior within an organization is studied in more groups that belong to the same generation.
Validity and generalization increase as the same generation is studied within several organizations and when the results of generation-characterizing behavior are compared to each other.

Sources: *Wat is onderzoek* (Nel Verhoeven, 2011). *Basisboek Methoden en Technieken* (Baarda en De Goede, 2001). *Mixing Methods in Psychology* (Todd, Nerlich, McKeown, Clarke, 2004). Part VI Visual Data, in Qualitative Research (ed. David Silverman, 2006).

The video summary of the process is also very useful when it comes to observing emotions. These emotions of the generation group provide information on the extent to which the members of the generation concerned are given the space and support they need from the other generations to integrate their updates into the surrounding organizational culture. Positive emotions and high energy in the group are signals of good conditions for the evolution of their culture. Negative emotions and a low level of energy are signals of stagnation in the evolution of the culture of their organization. As I mentioned several times: to renew outdated social patterns, a generation needs the openness and active support of the other generations.

From analyses to actions
The video summaries of all generations at an organization together create a realistic and lively scan of the actual culture and its evolutionary direction. It can be seen as an MRI scan of the organizational culture in motion. It shows the direction of the social evolution of the organization – the evolution of the culture – the speed of this evolutionary process, the barriers and the opportunities to improve the updating actions of each generation.

The generation video scans can be used for different purposes:

1. To raise the awareness of the updates of each generation.
2. To raise the awareness of the biggest energy drains for all generations, which is the effect of outdated social patterns in the culture.
3. To find new ways to support every generation in integrating their updates into the culture.

Creating awareness is one step, but really supporting the updating processes is another. A positive approach is very important, the focus on positive energy and on a positive collective goal: to keep your culture up to date as a way to improve its survival power.

When the different generations are aware of each other's updates, they can find ways together and with their managers to support each other in the updating processes.

1. Warming up	2. Working session with members of each generation	3. Analyzing and summarizing the video recordings	4. Multi-generation working session: shared analyses	5. Perseverance
Explaining the goal of the generational perspective + Fine-tuning the approach + Preparation of the sessions	7 to 9 members of each generation produce a top 5 of energizers and energy drains at work. All sessions are video-taped	Summarizing the updates/energizers of each generation and the outdated patterns/ energy drains on video and have it checked by the participants	All summaries together create a MRI scan of the current culture in motion: Direction of the evolution, the outdated patterns, the updating power of each generation. From this new perspective, new interventions can be found to support the updating processes.	Organizing supporting actions, proceeding from: Collaboration between generations at work + Management support + HR support

Duration of each phase:

(2 x) 2 hours	1.5 hours per session. 4 sessions in 1 day	One week	3 to 6 hours	Depends on actions

Total lead time is 2 to 4 weeks

Fig. 29 An overview of a generation approach

The analysis of the results and the process of deciding what action to take can be established together with all people concerned; together with all participants from generations, all managers and all HR professionals at once. This is an efficient way of working. People are able to get a lot of work done in a short period of time and the actions can be attuned to each other right away. Communal analysis and action creates a connection and a perceptible, collective strength. This phase can also be cut up into small parts: by drawing up an analysis with the participants of each generation, then with the formal leaders, and after that with HR, or going through the process first with a smaller part of the organization. The optimum course of action usually becomes clear during phase 1.

Even if people are really willing to make a change, the energy level is very high and the course of action is clear and unambiguous, do not underestimate the stubbornness of outdated cultural patterns. There is a good chance that the tendency to repeat these patterns remains strong. I would like to recommend continued support for the energizing developments and to follow them closely. Perhaps, separate interventions that strengthen each other need to be organized in order to allow the fresh patterns to be really integrated into the existing culture. The final purpose is to allow the generational influences to play a part in the process of collaboration and to keep the organization up to date by doing so.

Every fifteen years, a new generation enters a new phase of working life. The generational approach stimulates processes that lead to constant renewal, to constant updating processes in the organizational culture. This way of evolutionary renewal of a culture from within:

a Establishes a connection: between generations, between leaders and followers, between formal and informal leaders.

b Takes place in the process of collaboration, during the interaction between generations, and by supporting the generational strengths that are already present.

c Is a sustainable social process: new social patterns generate energy for all generations and when generations do what generates most energy at work they continually generate fresh social patterns. In this way, members of every generation keep on recharging their own 'human energy battery.'

d Stimulates employees' job satisfaction and self-confidence from the youngest to the oldest generation, because they are the ones renewing their own culture.

e Is a way to create continual social innovation by non-stop successive generations, which increases the possibilities of innovating services and products.

The management undergoes a function change as they shift from guiding the content of work performance of professionals towards supporting and facilitating their evolutionary power. This approach fits in well with the leadership style that is being developed by the new generation of Dutch leaders from the Connecting Generation X (see chapter 5). It also corresponds with the increasing need of professionals to influence their work and working environment to a higher extent.

As I mentioned before, the tendency of older generations to keep repeating outdated social patterns can remain persistent, because these have become a deep-rooted habit. In the decades to come, younger generations will be smaller than older generations at most of Dutch and other European organizations and institutions. This requires extra attention and support for the evolutionary strength of these 'minorities'. This implies also that new social patterns that generate work energy for all generations need to be supported and maintained for a certain period of time, as long as it takes people to integrate the new patterns into their existing repertoire, to the point of no return. The generational approach offers clear insight into the factors that deserve a bit of extra attention and perseverance and which will contribute to the process of updating an organization.

The fine-tuning of the generation approach

Every organization and every working community develops at its own evolutionary pace. Changing a culture too quickly, from one day to the other, produces nothing but chaos. Changing too slowly produces tension. It needs sensitivity, patience and complete openness from the ones who support the process.

This process of fine-tuning goes on differently in every organization. It depends on the existing culture. For example, when a certain organization has a dominant top-down culture, it might be necessary to focus first on the formal leaders and the informal leaders in every generation. In a separate session, the energizers of the formal leaders and their vision on the future of the company – the five key factors in creating a successful future – can be made. The videotaped results of this session can be compared with the results of the sessions with the informal leaders from each generation. The formal leaders will be given the opportunity to compare their own session results to the outcome of the sessions of the informal generation leaders. Usually, the results are more similar than they had expected beforehand. This strengthens the connection between the formal leaders and the informal leaders in the generations. Proceeding from this connecting strength, formal leaders and informal leaders from each generation will be able to achieve progress together. If the results of the sessions are not very similar to each other, this shows the reality of the situation. It may bring forth an interesting and important puzzle, which needs to be solved before the next step can be taken in the process.

Literature

About generations

Arsenault, P.M. (2004). 'Validating generational differences: A legitimate diversity and leadership issue'. *Leadership & Organization Development Journal*, 25, 124-141.

Bennis, W.G. & Thomas, R.J. (2002). *Geeks and Geezers. How era, values and defining moments shape leaders*, Harvard Business School Press, Boston.

Bontekoning, A.C. (2011). 'The evolutionary power of new generations'. *Psychology Research*, vol.1 no4.

Cennamo, L., & Gardner, D. (2008). 'Generational differences in work values, outcomes and person-organization values fit'. *Journal of Managerial Psychology*, 23, 891-906.

Cogin, J. (2012). 'Are generational differences in work values fact of fiction? Multi-country evidence and implications'. *The International Journal of Human Resource Management*, 23, 2268-2294.

Crampton, S.M., & Hodge, J.W. (2007). 'Generations in the workplace: Understanding age Diversity'. *The Business Review*, 9, 16-22.

Deal, J.J. (2007). *How Employees Young & Old Can Find Common Ground*. Jossey-Bass, San Francisco.

Dulin, L. (2008). 'Leadership preferences of Generation Y cohort: A mixed-methods investigation'. *Journal of Leadership Studies*, 2, 43-59.

Fredenburg, J. (2004). *Vision, the Answer to Generations X and Y*. Authorhouse, Bloomington.

Gibson, J.W., Greenwood, R.A., & Murphy, E.F. (2009). 'Generational differences in the workplace: Personal values, behaviors and popular beliefs'. *Journal of Diversity Management*, 4(3), 1-7.

Hicks, R. & Hicks, K. (1999). *Boomers, Xers and Other Strangers*. Tyndale House Publishers, Wheaton.

Joshi, A., Dencker, J. C., & Franz, G. (2011). 'Generations in organizations'. *Research in Organizational Behavior*, 31, 177-205.

Joshi, A., Dencker, J.C., Franz, G., & Martocchio, J.J. (2010).
'Unpacking generational identities in organizations'. *Academy of Management Review*, 35, 392–414.

Kowske, B.J., Rasch, R., & Wiley, J. (2010). 'Millennials' (lack of) attitude problem: An empirical examination of generational effects on work attitudes'. *Journal of Business and Psychology*, 25, 265-279.

Kunreuther, F., Kim, H. & Rodriguez, R. (2009). *Working across Generations*. Jossey-Bass, San Francisco.

Lancaster, L.C. & Stillmann, D. (2005). *When Generations Collide*. Collins Business, New York.

Mannheim, K. (1928). 'Das Problem der Generationen'. *Kölner Vierteljahrshefte für Soziologie*, VII, 2-3, pp.157-185 en (1929) 309-330.

Marías, J. (1970). *Generations, a Historical Method*. The University of Alabama Press, Alabama.

Martin, C.A. & Tulgan, B. (2001). *Managing Generation Y*. HRD Press, Amherst, MA.

Martin, C.A. & Tulgan, B. (2002). *Managing the Generation Mix*. HRD Press, Amherst, MA.

McGuire, D., By, R. T. & Hutchings, K. (2007). 'Towards a model of human resource solutions for achieving intergenerational interaction in organizations'. *Journal of European Industrial Training*, 31, 592-608.

Ortega y Gasset, J. (1923). *El tema de nuestro tiempo*. Rivesta de Occidente, Madrid.

Ortega y Gasset, J. (1993, original 1930). *The Revolt of the Masses*. W.W. Norton & Company, New York.

Ortega y Gasset, J. (2000, original 1953). *The Origin of Philosophy*. University of Illinois Press, Chicago.

Pfeffer, J. (1985). 'Organizational demography: Implications for management'. *California Management Review*, 28 (1), 67-81.

PWC. (2011). *Millennials at Work: Reshaping the Workplace*. Download http://www.pwc.nl/nl/publicaties/millennials-op-het-werk.html

Raines, C. (1997). *Beyond Generation X*. Crisp Publications, Menlo Park, CA.

Raines, C. & Hunt, J. (2000). *The Xers & the Boomers*. Thomson, Boston.

Raines, C. (2003). *Connecting Generations*. Crisp Publications, Menlo Park, CA.

Ralston, D.A. & Egri, C.P. (1999). 'Doing business in the 21th century with the new generation of Chinese managers: A study of generational shifts in work values in China'. *Journal of International Business Studies*, 30 (2), 415–427.

Sheehy, G. (1995). *New Passages. Mapping your life across time*. Ballantine Books, New York.

Strauss, W. & Howe, N. (1991). *Generations. The history of America's Future 1584-2069*. William Morrow, New York.

Strauss, W. & Howe, N. (1998). *The Fourth Turning*. Broadway Books, New York.

Strauss, W. & Howe, N. (2000). *Millennials Rising. The next great generation*. Vintage Books, New York.

Strauss, W. & Howe, N. (2006). *Millennials and the POP culture*. Life Course Associates, Great Falls (VA).

Tulgan, B. (1997). *Generation X*. HRD Press, Amherst, MA.

Tulgan, B. (2000). *Managing Generation X*. W.W. Norton & Company, London.

Zemke, R., Raines, C. & Filipczak, B. (2000). *Generations at work*, Amacom, New York.

Zurilla, T.J.D., Maydeu, A. & Kant, G. L. (1998). Age and gender differences in social problem-solving ability. *Personality and Individual Differences*, vol. 25, 241-152.

Dutch books and articles about generations:

Becker, H.A. (1992). *Generaties en hun kansen*. Meulenhoff, Amsterdam.

Becker, H.A. (1997). *De toekomst van de verloren generatie*. Meulenhoff, Amsterdam.

Bontekoning, A.C. (2008). 'Generaties als vernieuwingsimpulsen'. *M&O*, nr.1, 37-51.

Bontekoning, A.C. (2010). *'Het generatieraadsel. Ontdek de kracht van generaties'*. Mediawerf, Amsterdam.

Bontekoning, A.C. (2012). *Generaties! Werk in Uitvoering*. Mediawerf, Amsterdam.

Bontekoning, A.C. & Grondstra, M. (2012). *Ygenwijs*. Business Contact, Amsterdam.

Bontekoning, A.C. (2014). *Nieuwe generaties in vergrijzende organisaties*. Mediawerf, Amsterdam.

Boschma, J. & Groen, I. (2010). *Generatie Einstein, slimmer, sneller en volwassener*, Bruna Uitgevers, Utrecht.

Liempt van, P. & Gessel van, P. (2010). *Bye Bye Baby Boomers*. Business Contact, Amsterdam.

Diepstraten, I. , Ester, P. & Vinken, H. (1999). *Mijn generatie*. Syntax Publishers, Tilburg.

Nelis, H. (1999). *Jongeren als experts*, SMO, Den Haag.

Slageren van, I. & Steen van der, B. (2004). *Leiding geven aan dertigers*. Nelissen, Soest.

Spangenberg, F & Lampert, M. (2009). *De Grenzeloze Generatie*. Nieuw Amsterdam Uitgevers, Amsterdam.

Valk de, H.A.G. (2006). 'Op weg naar volwassenheid; niet-westerse allochtone en autochtone jongeren vergeleken'. *Demos, bulletin over bevolking en samenleving* 22(8): 73-76.

Wijnants, N. (2008). *Het dertigersdilemma*. Uitgeverij Bert Bakker, Amsterdam.

Other relevant books and articles:

Craeynest, P. (2005). *Psychologie van de levensloop.* Acco, Leuven.

Frijda, N.H. (1986). *The Emotions.* Cambridge University Press, Cambridge.

Gladwell, M. (2005). *Blink. The power of thinking without thinking.* Little, Brown and Company, New York.

Gladwell, M. (2008). *Outliers. The story of success.* Allen Lane, Penguin Group, London.

Goleman, D. (1995). *Emotional Intelligence.* Bantam Books, New York.

Gottman, J. (1993). *What Predicts Divorce. The relationship between marital processes and marital outcomes.* Academic Press, New York.

Hofstede, G. (2001). *Cultures Consequences.* Sage, London.

Karp, H., Fuller, C., Sirias, D. (2002). *Bridging the Boomer Xer Gap.* Davies-Black Publishers.

Knippenberg van, D., Dreu de, C.K.W. & Homan, A.C. (2004). 'Work Group Diversity and Group Performance'. *Journal of Applied Psychology* 89(6): 1008-1022.

Kotter, J.P. & Cohen, D.S. (2002). *The Heart of Change.* Harvard Business School Press, Boston.

Lamme, V. (2012) *De vrije wil bestaat niet.* Uitgeverij Bert Bakker, Amsterdam

Lau, D.C. & Murninghan, J.K. (2005). 'Interactions within groups and subgroups: the effects of demographic faultlines'. *Academy of Management Journal* 48(4): 645-659.

Latten, J.J. & Manting, D. (2006). 'Bevolkings- en allochtonenprognose: Nederland in 2025 sterk geprofileerd'. *Demos, bulletin over bevolking en samenleving* 22 (6): 54-57.

Lutz, W. (2007). 'Bevolkingsontwikkeling vergroot Europese identiteit op termijn; jongere generaties voelen zich thuis in EU'. *Demos, bulletin over bevolking en samenleving* 23(4): 1-4.

Meyerson, D.L. (2001). *Tempered Radicals.* Harvard Business School Press, Boston.

Mindell, A. (1995). *Sitting in the fire.* Lao Tse Press, Portland.

Mintzberg, H. (1989). *Mintzberg on Management.* Simon & Schuster, New York.

Martin, J. (1992). *Cultures in Organizations: Three perspectives.* Oxford University Press, New York.

Oppenhuisen, Joke (2000). *Een schaap in de bus?; een onderzoek naar waarden van de Nederlander.* Proefschrift. SWOCC, Amsterdam.

Quinn, R.E. (1996). *Deep Change,* Jossey-Bass, San Francisco.

Schein, E.H. (1999). *The Corporate Culture Survival Guide: Sense and nonsense about culture change.* Jossey-Bass Inc., San Francisco.

Senge, P. (1990). *The Fifth Discipline.* Doubleday, New York.

Senge, P., Scharmer, C.O., Jaworski, J. & Flowers, B.S. (2005). *Presence: Exploring profound change in people, organizations and society.* Nicholas Brealey Publishers, London.

Swaab, D. (2014). *We are our Brains.* Spiegel & Grau, New York.

Thornton, W.J.L. & Dumke, H.A. (2005). 'Age differences in Everyday Problem-Solving and Decision-Making'. *Psychology and Ageing,* vol.30, no.1, 85-99.

Vaughan, F.E. (1979). *Awakening Intuition.* Anchor Press, New York.

Aart Bontekoning

Aart Bontekoning has developed his own unique expertise in the field of generations that succeed each other in life stages and have evolutionary powers to keep the organizations and teams they are part of up to date. As an organizational psychologist and generation expert he supports evolutionary change processes with successive generations at organizations. He is a popular speaker and shares his knowledge and experience through master classes and public speeches.

As a researcher, he is still improving his unique generation research method. He supervises (doctoral) students who are doing (complementary) generational research and has authored various articles and books about the evolutionary power of generations in organizations. Many companies, governmental institutions and educational institutions draw on his insights and services.

Aart Bontekoning was born on a farm in West Friesland, in the north of the Netherlands. He spent his childhood days in a typical Dutch polder. His career started early, as he joined the Dutch police force at age nineteen. He started as a street cop and later became a member of the manage-

ment team. It was in management that his fascination for the dynamics of processes of change came to the surface, prompting him to decide to study organizational psychology at Utrecht University when he was 32. Five years later, he graduated and left the police force. He worked for a consultancy for a few years and decided to start a career as an independent consultant in 1990.

Around 1993, he noticed that remarkably many well-educated young professionals, members of the first cohorts of the Pragmatic Generation (1970-1985), started losing their fresh views, ideas and work energy shortly after starting their careers. This was the start of a long quest for Aart. As he conducted experiments, he tried to explore the causes of this development and the possible interventions to solve the problem. You can read more about this period in chapters 12 and 13.

Between 2000 and 2007, he studied the influence generations have on the development of organizational cultures (the collective 'working intelligence' of organizations) more profoundly. This scientifically explorative journey led him to surprising results. He discovered there was no clear

generation theory developed yet, and no scientific research
had ever been done in this field. He developed and tested
a generational theory and a unique research method. In
2007, he obtained his doctoral degree for the results of his
research in the Netherlands. From that time on the popularity of his generation approach has increased strongly. Not
least because his approach provides answers for the many
(Dutch) aging organizations and institutions that want to
know how they can keep 'up to date'. At the same time this
creates opportunities to deepen and expand his generation
research.

In this book, he takes his research to the next level: starting
from a generational theory, he continues to optimally exploit
the cultural, renewing strength of all working generations.
Based on the Dutch case.

For more information: www.aartbontekoning.com/en